What Makes This Day Different?

What Makes This Day Different?

Preaching Grace on Special Occasions

David J. Schlafer

Cowley Publications
CAMBRIDGE, MASSACHUSETTS

Library of Congress Cataloging-in-Publication Data:
Schlafer, David J., 1944–
    What makes this day different?: preaching grace on special occasions / David J. Schlafer.
       p.   cm.
ISBN 10: 1-56101-156-8   ISBN 13: 978-1-56101-156-8   (alk. paper)
1. Preaching. 2. Occasional services. 3. Fasts and feasts. I. Title.
BV4221.S28 1998
251—dc21   98-13942
                                                                CIP

This book is printed on recycled, acid-free paper and was produced in the United States of America.

Second Printing

Cowley Publications   •   *4 Brattle Street*
Cambridge, Massachusetts 02138
800-225-1534   •   *www.cowley.org*

For
Eugene Lowry
and
O. C. Edwards, Jr.

preaching visionaries
treasured friends

Contents

Acknowledgments

Preaching is a gloriously collegial enterprise. I am grateful to the colleagues whose sermon efforts have enriched this preaching conversation, and who have graciously given permission for their sermons to be included on the following pages in this volume.

Kevin Kelly (43)
Stephen Casey (55-56)
Ruth Frey (69-70)
Katherine Moorehead (71-72)
Tom Sramek, Jr. (82)
Katharine Jefferts Schori (89-91)
Larry Walters (106-107)
Don Wardlaw (111-114)
Michael Moore (122-125)
Bonnie Joia Roddy (137-140)
Margaret Faeth (152-154)
James Adams (154-157)

Writing is not done in isolation, either. Cynthia Shattuck and Vicki Black of Cowley Publications, as always, have helped it happen, and I honor their efforts as well.

PART I

Special Occasions as
"Grace-Catchers"

CHAPTER ONE

What Brings Us Together Today?

"What makes this night different from all other nights?" The question has been ritually asked by generations of Jewish children at the yearly celebration of Passover. "What makes this day different?" An answer to that question is also what Christians seek in a sermon on a special occasion. Not every day is an ordinary day. There are a number of days on which homiletical "business as usual" is not what is called for. We always gather to celebrate and seek the grace of God, but we do not always do so in the same way. Different concerns come to the fore at different times.

How does God's love touch our births and our deaths, our marriage vows and our ordination vows, our high holy days and our civic holidays? How is God's grace manifest in the lives of those whom the church calls "saints"? How does grace touch troublesome social and theological issues that tear at the fabric of our common life? Is there a word from the Lord in the midst of nagging problems that lead to deepening anxiety or disasters that suddenly descend? How can we use retreats, preaching missions, and liturgical seasons to help each other awaken to God's presence in fresh and creative ways? How can guest preachers create a new word when they "pinch hit" for the local pastor?

These are all quite different questions, but they are also variations on the same question: *how does the preacher frame, from the richly textured Word of God, a word that speaks to the distinctive event that brings individuals together on this particular day?* How can sermons for special occasions serve as places for God's people to pause and consider changes in life's direction as they attempt to hear and to follow God's call? The need for a unified yet nuanced approach to special occasion preaching is a pressing one. When major life transitions are uppermost in the minds of our congregations, they may well be more open to a hearing of the gospel than they are on ordinary days:

- ∾ "Why did God let Grandma die? I thought God loved me!"
- ∾ "How will I get through Easter after the hell of my divorce?"
- ∾ "What does St. Anselm have to do with life in the twenty-first century?"
- ∾ "How will we ever manage to bring up the child we baptize today?"
- ∾ "Surely this marriage will last—by God, we'll *make* it last!"
- ∾ "I really need this retreat, but what am I supposed to do with it?"
- ∾ "Why do I have to get ashes on my forehead tonight? I feel like dirt already!"
- ∾ "Why must we do a brass band blessing of our rotten government on the Fourth of July?"

These questions are not casual; the energy behind them is palpable. They indicate significant turning points, critical junctures, in the lives of those who ask them—what I call "mark points" in the life of the church or community. On these tragic, joyful, or festive occasions we do not have to capture a congregation's attention, for we already have it. It is our duty and privilege on such occasions to direct our congregation's attention to God's pillar of cloud and fire that can transform a people's wilderness wandering into purposeful ventures toward a land of promise. A special occasion sermon is not a way of pandering to jaded palates or a ploy to catch people out at a moment of vulnerability. A special occasion sermon is a word fitly spoken. When it is not, or when the concern of the day is poorly addressed, the effect of the sermon can be worse than if the occasion were not mentioned at all. Expectations raised and then thwarted become a source of deep and continuing frustration.

I shall never forget a seminary homiletics course I once convened that focused on the problem of evil. It first explored various theodicies systematically, then invited students to test them out by preaching sermons addressed to hypothetical congregations on various occasions of crisis. Although it was not part of the assignment, almost all the students preached the sermons that they had needed to hear at a critical point in their lives—but did not hear because the preacher on that occasion failed to address the situation, or addressed it badly. Homiletical opportunities for a fitly spoken word are often lost opportunities. The critical moment passes, but the deep need remains.

Faced with the challenge of holding up one facet of grace that is unique to a particular occasion, many preachers instinctively shrink from it. Their justifications are legion:

- ∾ "The couple doesn't hear anything in the wedding ceremony anyway."
- ∾ "The reading of the passion gospel on Palm Sunday is a sermon in itself."
- ∾ "Nobody wants to hear a history lecture on a saint's day."

- "You can't really address fresh grief effectively in a sermon."
- "The church isn't the place to celebrate secular holidays."
- "The pulpit isn't the place to deal with controversial issues."
- "People won't come for church services several nights in a row."
- "You can't do much good as a guest preacher—you don't know the people."

And what are the sermons we often *do* hear on such occasions?

- exhortations to uncritical patriotism on civic holidays ;
- put-downs of worshipers who show up only on Christmas or Easter;
- treatises on ethics or ecclesiology at weddings;
- Hallmark card sentimentalities at funerals;
- guilt-trips on Ash Wednesday, and gory details on Good Friday.

It is one thing to wax indignant at such misuses of the preaching office, but it is something else to take on the task of addressing the full spectrum of special occasion sermons. Each occasion must be spoken to and be allowed to speak on its own behalf. Yes, of course, but with how *much* of a voice, and what *kind*? Is there a broad vision, or at least some guidelines, that we can use in shaping such preaching? Are there predictable problem areas, and ways to confront them? Do certain sermon techniques work better on some occasions than on others?

Questions like these come up repeatedly in the course of a preaching ministry. The occasions that prompt them, however, often arise without warning. There is little time to reflect on the theology and practice of funeral preaching when the tearful telephone call snaps us suddenly awake in the middle of the night. Even when we can see the preaching event coming from a distance, as on Easter or Christmas, questions concerning how to prepare the sermon often get pushed to the sidelines. We have to produce the sermon (along with attending to a thousand other holiday things) but we do not have time to stop and think how best to go about it!

⌔ *What is "High Time"?*

Someone unfamiliar with preaching might easily get the impression that a sermon is a religious monologue, but that is a misperception. Preaching is conversation, a sacred conversation in which many voices take part—the voices of scripture, culture, congregation, and preacher. The particular concerns of the day are still another voice in the conversation. A wedding, a saint's day, a high holy day, or a secular holiday also need a place in the dialogue. How can we give these special occasion voices a proper hearing? How, homiletically, can faith be realized in the midst of *this* occasion?

In beginning to think about this question, I find it helpful to return to a distinction that is often made in theology courses, the distinction between *kairos* and *chronos*. Both are ways of marking time. *Chronos* time is "clock and calendar" time, marked by regular, mathematical signposts. It is the same for everyone, regardless of its importance for any individual. Significant events are often tagged by reference to the clock ("Sally was born at 5:32 A.M. on Tuesday, November 26, 1997"), but the time itself has no significance. When people do not experience anything particularly unusual or important over an extended period, they often describe themselves as merely "marking time."

Yet marking time can also have a different connotation. *Kairos,* or "high time," comes when events converge at a point of profound significance. *Kairos* time is an occasion that marks a definite and perhaps definitive shift in the life trajectory of a person or community. It may come at a point of deliberate choice ("I took the road less traveled by/ And that has made all the difference") or it may catch us up suddenly in a swirl of events over which we seem to have no control ("The phone call came, announcing that the company was filing for bankruptcy, and our lives were upended"). *Kairos* may come upon us all at once or dawn upon us slowly and almost imperceptibly, its full impact recognized only in retrospect. In either case, *kairos* is a time of distinctive life-shaping. We mark such times precisely because we experience ourselves as being marked *by* them.

Not every decision point is a *kairos* point, but failure to recognize it when it comes can have momentous implications. The challenge for the preacher on such occasions, therefore, is to mark time as high time—to offer a sermon that has reasonable prospects of "seizing the day." Educators sometimes talk about "teachable moments," those points in the learning process when we are ready and able to "get it." Such moments do not just happen; they have to be prepared for and picked up on. Nor can they be manufactured or imposed: if there is anything worse than ignoring a special occasion in a sermon, it is using the sermon as an attempt to force a *kairos* experience on cue. Practical sermon strategies for effecting such an outcome simply do not work.

Major mark points in life are often described as being "peak" or "mountain top" experiences. There is often a fascinating, liminal quality about them. People facing life-threatening disease, for example, often report a powerful, almost luminous dimension to that critical time in their lives. Often the meaning of the experience cannot be put into words, nor can its full meaning be grasped all at once: it took Julian of Norwich twenty years to appropriate the mystical visions she received within the space of a few hours.

8

The task of the preacher at such times is to explore, but not to explain: to illuminate the mystery without eliminating it. Neither the special occasion sermon itself, nor the distinctive awareness of God that it intends to foster, is the end point of a journey into God, or even a spotlight on a certain segment of the path. It is more like a floodlight or a lantern, shedding illumination on the surrounding territory and providing orientation and ongoing direction for a movement into what is still unknown.

To use another metaphor, a special occasion sermon is a kind of punctuation. The regular Sunday sermon provides periods, commas, and semicolons in our religious life texts; the special occasion sermon supplies the question marks, exclamation points, quotation marks—and dashes! Or to shift metaphors again, perhaps sermons in ordinary time are like bar lines designating measures in a musical score, while sermons on special occasions are like accent marks, or markings indicating changes in tempo and mood.

A definition of "special occasion" may be helpful at this point. Whether it is happy or sad, the situation for which this kind of sermon is called is an occasion of *celebration* (whether formal or informal, joyful or tragic) where people *come together* ("celebrating alone" is a misnomer) to make a *"big deal"* about a significant *event or relationship*. It is a situation where words *fitly spoken* enhance everyone's experience of the occasion. How does that definition play itself out in real life? We have all been at weddings or retirement dinners, I suspect, where the occasion cried out for words from the best man, the family matriarch, or the boss that would sum up with a certain grace the warm sentiments everyone shared—and yet the opportunity was lost or muffed. We felt let down, empty, a bit disoriented, and to some extent isolated from those around us. We have all gathered around the television during times of national crisis or tragedy, aching for a word of collective outrage, comfort, or direction, only to be disappointed.

On other such occasions, however, the spoken words were memorable—not necessarily lengthy or flowery, but memorable. Franklin D. Roosevelt's "Day of Infamy" speech or Neil Armstrong's "One small step for man" are at one end of the spectrum. At the other are the thoughtful expressions of gratitude by a daughter at the fiftieth wedding anniversary of her parents, or a mother's word of realistic assurance in the midst of family tragedy. I remember fondly a plainsong "psalm" chant, composed expecially for me and sung at a surprise farewell party given by a small group of students as I took leave of one institution for a job at another. Such words capture our sentiments and provide a context for our joy or our anguish. They send us forth renewed and energized even though we may have arrived frayed and exhausted, setting aside already overloaded schedules in order to attend.

Good special occasion sermons convene such celebrations in the communal life of the people of God. A special occasion sermon works *together* with its occasion, lifting up the day's significance. When it is effective, the sermon also highlights the potential for a teachable moment in the day without turning the occasion into a didactic classroom exercise. How does a preacher give this special occasion a proper voice in the sound of the sermon? How can the high times of life be shaped as illuminating mark points in our sermons, rather than turned into "high points" in a religious lecture or a sentimental homily? That is the question to which we will turn next.

CHAPTER TWO

How Much of a Voice, and What Kind?

When we fail to celebrate the significance of the situation in the sermon of the day, we commit the homiletical equivalent of ignoring the elephant in the living room. We treat what nobody can possibly avoid looking at as though it simply were not there. The voice of the occasion will relentlessly press its claim, however, demanding to be acknowledged. When preachers turn a deaf ear to this voice, they create a condition in which "the stones will cry out," as Jesus says to the Pharisees who want to silence the crowd's "hosannas" on his triumphal entry into Jerusalem.

Yet becoming obsessed with the special occasion is certainly no better than ignoring it. Confronted with a day of particular significance, preachers sometimes resort to homiletical overkill. That is unfortunate, because a sermon crammed full of seemingly relevant observations and timely applications can easily distort the congregation's hearing of the gospel. All the sermon's special flourishes can distract attention from the very situation toward which they are trying to point.

It is not terribly difficult to identify either of these extremes in the abstract, or to prescribe the happier, middle-of-the road alternative: "Not too little attention, not too much—just the right amount!" That advice, of course, is as unhelpful as it is obvious. How much is enough? How large a role should the occasion play in the drama of the sermon? But, obvious though they seem, these may not be the most helpful questions to ask. Approaching this homiletical challenge with a quantitative, "more or less" mindset is not likely to prove very fruitful. Nor is the task simply a matter of artistic proportion, or of giving "equal time" in the sermon conversation to the various voices of scripture, congregation, culture, preacher, and the occasion itself. What we need here is a coherent theological and homiletical vision.

What are the alternatives that are open to the preacher? I suggest the following as a point of departure: the preacher who does not deal directly with the occasion is talking *around* it, and the preacher who is inordinately preoccupied with the situation talks *about* it, or *at* it. The more viable alternative is to preach *through* the situation. Let me flesh out the distinctions I have in mind.

⌘ *Preaching Around the Occasion*

It is possible to preach *around* a special occasion in one of two ways: either by ignoring it altogether, or by dealing with issues at the periphery of the situation, rather than at its heart. With respect to homiletical avoidance, however, leading one's listeners on a sermon detour around the issue is not always done without forethought. A reasonable case can be made for resisting "the tyranny of the immediate" by refusing to address the occasion altogether, or by acknowledging it with only the most cursory nod.

Why might a preacher adopt such a strategy? Because to make every front page headline the centerpiece of a special occasion sermon—whether the news is political, ecclesiastical, or personal—is to cheapen and even betray a sense of the relevance of the gospel. Karl Barth once suggested that God's response to what we human beings regard as the burning question of the day is: "Wrong question!" That observation is not one to be easily dismissed. Agenda-driven preaching is a dangerous enterprise. God cannot be simply defined as "The One Who Meets Our Special Needs," or "The One Who Expects Behavior X as Proof of Our Discipleship."

Barth's warning is well taken. Yet some situations raise issues of ultimate concern so forcefully that to ignore them in the sermon is to take a serious risk. God may not be the fixer of situations or the issuer of marching orders, but if people cannot discern God's particular presence or call at critical times in their lives, they may not have much interest in finding or hearing God at any other time, either.

Precisely what constitutes such a "critical time," of course, is to some extent a pastoral judgment call, not unlike the decision every preacher must make about how a particular special occasion should be handled in the sermon. The death of an eighty-year-old mother, for instance, may or may not be traumatic for her children; the preacher must decide accordingly whether or not an expression of lament will be integral to the funeral sermon. In similar fashion, a hotel fire halfway around the world, the imminent approach of Labor Day, the feast of St. Dunstan—any of these may or may not be a "special occasion" that merits explicit focus or extended treatment in a sermon. In any case, the decision is one that the preacher needs to wrestle with. To preach or not to preach upon a special occasion cannot in advance be answered: "Not!"

Fully aware that the principle could be misapplied, I would suggest that the presumption should be "Preach it!"—at least to the extent of seriously reflecting on what the possibilities might entail. Preaching *around* a significant occasion is seldom a good move. A special occasion focus might even be called for during apparently ordinary times—perhaps urgently called for. The ordinary rhythms of everyday life sometimes feel monotonous and predictable. During such periods, people can easily lose a sense of how their lives are at every point undergirded by God's all-embracing presence. Deliberately making a "big deal" in a sermon on a saint's day, a congregational event (such as the commissioning of church school teachers), or a regular cultural observance (such as the city's annual water sports carnival) might be a most effective way of evoking in one's listeners a fresh sense of God's grace in the midst of the mundane. Sermon hearers need, with Jacob, to discover again and again "How awesome is this place. Surely the Lord is in this place and we did not know it."

Preaching around a special occasion may not mean avoiding it altogether; it may mean skirting around it—coming within range, but not pressing into the center. This is the "red herring" approach: using bogus arguments that distract the hearer from the heart of the matter by talking about something peripheral to it. Preaching generally, and special occasion preaching in particular, often follows a diversionary path with red herrings like these:

- ∾ Is the return of spring relevant to celebrating Christ's resurrection? Yes and no.
- ∾ Are the sentiments of "America, the Beautiful" expressions of responsible Christian commitment on occasions of civic significance? Well....
- ∾ Are the sparkles of romance so evident in the marriage rite the appropriate stuff of a wedding sermon? Maybe so, but then again, maybe not—at least no more than the nostalgia of "home again for Christmas" is the proper center for a celebration of the Incarnation.
- ∾ What is the response of a faithful Christian community to abortion? "Right to life" and "freedom of choice," at

least as played out in the public arena, are also homiletical "red herrings."

∿ Preaching About the Occasion

If preaching *around* the special occasion ignores or skirts the issue, preaching *about* the situation makes the opposite mistake. It pays the situation too much of the wrong kind of attention.

Preaching *about* the situation often takes place when the occasion is a saint's day celebration or a high holy day (Easter, Christmas, Ash Wednesday, or Maundy Thursday), a secular holiday (Thanksgiving, Mother's Day, or Memorial Day), a financial crisis in the parish, or a complex social dilemma with unsettling political implications (such as the national debt, or the role of the United States in an international dispute). The preacher delivers a sermon that is a theological information package. It informs the faithful about the issue before the house and may suggest, in light of this information, a general stance of moral virtue, or a specific amendment of life. This kind of "about" preaching also happens at weddings and funerals when the sermon becomes a treatise on "the sanctity of the marriage vow" or "the reality of life everlasting in God's many mansions."

There may well be a need for the dissemination of information on these occasions, but a worship service is singularly ill-suited for the transfer of extensive information. Few special occasions are conducive to the assimilation of factual or conceptual data. A sermon "about" the issues of the day, furthermore, is seldom a sermon that evokes fresh, direct awareness of the God who is present to us, here, at this time and place. The highly personal dimension of grace is critical in special occasion preaching. Those who are being wed, buried, or ordained are not simply instances of married life, human mortality, or recipients of holy orders. There is something more personal at stake on this Fourth of July than "the responsibilities of all Christian citizens," on this Ash Wednesday than "all flesh is grass," and "all have sinned." The "about" sermon loses this personal focus. When looking at a group photograph, we instinctively scan it, asking: "Where am I in this picture?" Similarly, in a special occasion sermon, listeners will be asking, even if unconsciously, "Is there a word in all of this for me?" The "about" sermon seldom tells them. The "at" sermon does—probably more than they want or need to hear.

౿ Preaching At the Occasion

This kind of preaching usually takes place when the occasion is a pastoral office, such as a wedding, funeral, or confirmation, or a local crisis involving personal disagreements. Such an occasion calls for comfort, encouragement, advice, or admonition, the preacher reasons: "People have a need for spiritual 'goods' and it is my job to deliver them." So the preacher tries to deliver—with instruction to the confirmands, marching orders to a disheveled or conflicted congregation, or endless pontifications on "what we all know you are feeling right now" to the soon-to-be married or the recently bereaved. The intention is usually well-meant, yet by preaching so explicitly to the presumed concerns of those in attendance, the preacher is preaching both *at* the occasion and *at* the people primarily involved. This kind of preaching often "hits its mark"—and that is precisely its problem.

Sermons are forms of public address, not private counseling or calling-on-the-carpet sessions aimed at a chosen few, with the rest of the congregation listening in. It is little wonder that much well-intended preaching at the situation achieves exactly the opposite of its desired effect.

Who of us can actually hear, let alone take in, private words delivered in a public forum? What couple will hear God's word for them on their wedding day if that word is nothing more than moral advice or allusions to tender places in their private lives that have been the subject of premarital counseling sessions? What grieving family will be grateful if the preacher kindly but bluntly pokes around their already open wounds in the funeral homily, or if their deceased relative is eulogized as a figure larger (and better) than life? And pity the poor ordinand and those who gather to celebrate with her! They are likely to receive a sermon payload that is delivered from both barrels at once: "The priesthood is in serious trouble. Consider the low regard for clergy, and the low concern for religion in this day and age. You are in for a lonely, thankless, but essential task. In order to bear this heavy burden, you must...."

Whether the situation becomes an occasion for general information or moral exhortation, those who come to the preaching banquet are sent away simultaneously stuffed and starved—they receive at once too much, and not enough. In sermons that preach *about* the occasion, the situation itself becomes an object of reflection; in sermons that preach *at* the occasion, those who have most at stake are singled out as objects of attention. Neither form of homiletical "objectivity" tends to be very fruitful. What is the alternative? Preaching *through* the special occasion.

∾ Preaching Through the Occasion

Preaching *through* the special occasion means, first of all, being sensitive to the history behind the event being celebrated, and to the possible futures it opens up. This does not mean that the sermon must follow the situation from beginning to end, laboriously tracking every detail—retelling the visit of the magi to the Christ child or the brave women to the empty tomb on Easter morning, telling the life-story of the deceased, recounting the courtship of the couple getting married, or giving a blow-by-blow account of the current parish crisis. Nor will the sermon issue detailed maps of the joys and struggles on the road ahead.

A special occasion sermon should, however, be sensitive to the movement and flow of the particular situation. The open-ended, journeying quality of which the celebration is a mark point is precisely what generates the higher-than-usual interest on the particular occasion. The sermon, then, will catch, incorporate, and engage listeners with the plot of this out-of-the-ordinary experience.

Preaching *through* the special occasion will also mean using the occasion as a homiletical "window" for the sermon. It is a way of providing fresh vision, new perspective, on the ever-present, all-surrounding grace of God. The occasion will be that *through* which, rather than *upon* which, the sermon is focused.

The distinguished preacher Phillips Brooks claimed that the personality of the preacher is the essential interpretive "grid" through which any effective sermon must pass. Why? Not just because such sermons are interesting, but because they are incarnational. God's fullest self-revelation, Brooks asserted, occurred in the particular life of Jesus of Nazareth. If God's loving communication took place in flesh and blood, a sermon that is disconnected from the personality of its preacher will seriously misrepresent the gospel. That is why our sermons cannot simply tell people that because God came to humankind once upon a time in Palestine, the divine presence is therefore available to all human beings in all places and times. We have to help people see *how*, not simply inform them *that*, God is present here and now. Helping listeners grasp how God's love is distinctively manifest through the life of a saint, in the midst of a troubling disagreement, in the silence shaped by a retreat meditation, in the tragic conditions of a death, in the joyful occasion of a wedding, in the unlikely event of a secular holiday—that is the goal toward which the special occasion sermon needs to strive.

The perspective can be from the other direction as well. What does it mean to see my ordination, our church's celebration of new ministry, the annual celebration of Memorial Day, or the wounds brought by those assembled at this liturgy of healing in the light of the scripture texts we read on this day? Sensitively interpreted, the scriptures may offer not a lesson to be learned or a moral to be applied, but rather a whole new window through which to look at our special condition in the light of eternity. Scripture may provide a window on what makes this day different, and the occasion may even help us to see the scriptures themselves in fresh perspective. The ultimate impact of such preaching will extend far beyond the setting of the particular occasional sermon. If those who hear a sermon can see how God is present to them, perhaps unexpectedly, through *this* time and place, their imaginations will be stretched and sparked to see for themselves the constant grace of God in other times and places as well.

So the question "How much of a voice should the situation have?" needs to be reframed as "What strategies are needed so that grace may be heard through this situation?" What *kind* of a voice does it have? A voice that mediates and goes between, using language that draws the listener not *to* but *through* its window on the occasion.

❧ *Occasional Sermons as "Grace-Catchers"*

My wife and I have a small but growing collection of individually crafted prisms made of leaded glass. Some are geometrical shapes, some are stars, some are animals and sea creatures. Each refracts a different pattern of light when placed in line with the rays of the sun. The vivid colors that these prisms throw upon the wall are not, of course, created *de novo* by the angles of the cut glass or "put" into the prisms by the artist who cut them. The brilliance and the color spectrum have been present (though undifferentiated) in the sunlight all along. Through meticulous artistry, the particular cuts of the prisms sharply focus distinctive light rays, and send them shimmering in particular directions. Such prisms are commonly called "sun-catchers."

Like these prisms, the well-shaped special occasion sermon is, I think, a "grace-catcher." Through the artistry of the preacher, it selects and focuses colors from the spectrum of God's grace both through and for the particular special occasion.

A fundamental question remains, however: what does it mean in practical terms to preach *through* a special occasion? Most of us, like my students in the "problem of evil" class, can probably recall the frustration, even the anguish, of situations in which the preacher sermonized *around* an occasion that cried out to be honored. Chances are we can also remember hearing sermons in which the occasion was preached *about,* or sermons in which we were offended (or deeply embarrassed for someone else who was offended) by a sermon preached *at* an occasion. But those times when we have heard a situation preached *through* may be harder to remember—and that for one of two reasons. Either we have not heard very many, or we were so engaged by the sermon that we were oblivious to the homiletical artistry that gave it shape. We were there as sermon receivers, rather than as practitioners of the craft.

If we have been graced with such sermons, some reflection on what made them effective is in order. The rest of this book will offer a framework for that reflection. We will talk about strategies and techniques that can help our special occasion sermons serve as "grace-catchers," and look at several examples of special occasion sermons. What you will probably find is that, once we get down to cases, you will be able to recall some of the positive examples of your previous sermon experiences in surprising detail. While the strategies employed by their preachers were not ostentatious, or even obvious, they were definite and effective.

But that is getting slightly ahead of the game. First, we need to consider this question: in what specific situations do we need to preach special occasion sermons? When is it "high time" to preach an occasional sermon? Not any time the preacher thinks it would be nice to have a little variety. Not in response to a worry that the troops may be getting restless, nor in reaction to every "squeaky wheel" or special interest group. Rather, "high times" are those occasions when the days of our lives seem to call out with special urgency for sacred shaping.

When do such times tend to occur? And what, precisely, is it about such times that enable us to recognize them as occasions that need to have a special focus? It is easier to give examples of these occasions than it is for us to articulate just what it is that makes them special. Getting a feel for the distinguishing characteristics of different mark points and high times will not in and of itself prepare any sermons for us, but it may save us from some false starts and give us some direction. As we shall see, each type of sermon has its own challenges and possibilities, yet there is an underlying similarity in all of their variety.

CHAPTER THREE

When is It "High Time"?

What occasions in the flow of a community's life can become effective preaching prisms? Are there common features that might help us in coming up with fitting words for various high times? I can think of several ways to categorize special occasions:

- ∾ Some special occasions are *momentous* ("really" special), while others seem *less significant*.
- ∾ Some special occasions are *joyful*, while others are *somber* or emotionally *neutral*.
- ∾ Some special occasions are *one-time events*, while others are *recurrent*.
- ∾ Some special occasions focus on the lives of particular *individuals*, others on the corporate history and shared life of a religious *community*, and still others on the life and history of the surrounding *culture*.

What implications do these distinctions have for preaching? Let's look at each one in turn.

∾ Momentous and Less Significant Occasions
Liturgical churches commonly speak of "major feast days." The Episcopal Church has a book of appointed prayers and scripture lessons (together with brief historical references and

theological reflections) called *Lesser Feasts and Fasts* that distinguishes between "major holy days" and "lesser" ones. The distinction is obvious, helpful, and has a certain transfer value to other preaching situations where pastoral and cultural concerns are more prominent. The fact is that some days *are* more extraordinary than others.

Mother's Day, Labor Day, or the feast day designated for Cuthbert of Lindisfarne—probably none of these are days on which we will suspend liturgical business as usual. A clear and gentle sermon nod is surely sufficient; anything grander would be like dressing up in formal attire for a casual Friday night fish fry. On the other hand, we make a big deal out of Christmas and Easter, weddings and funerals. Days of great importance in the life of the church are paralleled by days of significant life transition for individuals—baptisms, marriages, and funerals. A perfunctory sermon recognition on any such occasion would be a failure to mark the event as decisively as the event marks us.

Some events clearly fall in the middle of this spectrum. Epiphany, All Saints' Day, feasts of the original apostles, Thanksgiving Day, the day of a confirmation—a "deep bow," homiletically speaking, seems more in order on such occasions than a slight nod or a genuflection. Regardless of where the occasion falls along the spectrum, moreover, there are other dynamics the preacher must consider. Big days often carry high expectations as well as ambivalent memories of past occasions when, for whatever reasons, these high expectations were not met. The attention of those who assemble for celebration is probably primed on momentous occasions. Yet primed attention is not necessarily well-focused attention. An eager appetite is not necessarily a discerning appetite.

Preaching on momentous occasions has great possibilities; it can also be precarious. While a momentous occasion must be honored in the sermon, it does not follow that the only way, or even the best way, to acknowledge the richness is with preaching that is ornate. A sermon might be all the more effective for being subtle. A more down-to-earth occasion may sometimes be a better preaching prism than a momentous occasion. The intersection of heightened interest and somewhat modest expectations is not a bad place to stand, if one is the preacher of the day.

Distinguishing between major and minor feasts can be helpful for preaching on a special occasion, but this way of dividing the homiletical territory also has drawbacks. What makes an occasion momentous depends a lot on who and where the particular listeners are; what counts as significant is influenced by the training, temperament, and circumstances of those to whom the sermon is addressed. Cuthbert's feast, for example, is a momentous occasion when it is celebrated by the inhabitants of Lindisfarne. To say that an occasion is momentous does not tell us *for whom*, or *in what ways*. It may be appropriate, therefore, to consider another way of categorizing special occasions, one that focuses more on the listener than on the event.

○⤳ *Joyful, Somber, and Neutral Occasions*

Weddings, baptisms, ordinations, celebrations of new ministries, Easter, Christmas, Thanksgiving—it is a safe bet that most people will arrive at the church on such occasions with smiles on their faces. If tears are shed on these days, they will probably be tears of joy. That tells the preacher something. If the sermon casts a gray cloud over the proceedings—going on about high divorce rates at a wedding, lecturing about declining church participation at baptisms, railing against commercialism on Christmas Eve—it should hardly be surprising if the congregation departs disgruntled. Even if the preacher feels that he or she should do more on such occasions than give the people what they want, it does not nullify the obligation to meet the people where they are. As preachers we may need to do more than uplift the spirit of the occasion, but surely we can do no less.

The same can be said for the different moods surrounding funerals, services like Ash Wednesday and Good Friday, or days in which the focus of the occasion is conflict, crisis, or struggle. The reality of the resurrection may need to be preached on such occasions, but the preacher cannot stop there. Deep trouble or serious moral accountability must be addressed as well as joy. The tears that flow on somber occasions may need to be dried, but in a rather different way than on more joyful ones.

But then there are days on which no tears are very likely—days when people come to church with neither palpable joy nor crushing grief. A saint's day? So what else is new? Pentecost? That's nice. Independence Day or Memorial Day? Must we really? Unless the community is deeply engaged in the liturgical life of the church, or there is a large contingent of veterans or military personnel in the congregation, there is often little here for the preacher to pick up and run with on these days. That fact in itself is worth attending to.

It is helpful to classify sermons by the feelings of those who will hear them on a given occasion, but there is a downside to this as well. Strong emotions are mixed throughout the congregation as a whole. Christmas has a painful side for many people, and not all funerals are occasions of anguish. If we treat special occasions primarily as sad days or glad days, the result may well be superficial sermons. Is there, then, a more sophisticated way in which to envision special occasions?

❧ *One-Time Events and Recurring Observances*

The feelings displayed at weddings, funerals, baptisms, and ordinations are usually quite different. Yet those preaching situations have this in common: the gathering is occasioned by a single event in the faith/life cycle of the people involved. While we often remember the anniversaries of such events, the events themselves are one-time occurrences. Thanksgiving, Christmas, Easter, Memorial Day, and saint's days are annual observances. They are more akin to birthday celebrations than to celebrations of a birth. An event being remembered is different from an event being enacted live. The preacher's task at an annual remembrance is to foster a sense of immediacy and connection with someone or some event "once upon a time." The challenge of the sermon at the one-time event is complementary: to honor the immediate occasion, but to place it in broader perspective as well.

Yet this distinction can be overdrawn. Part of the energy surrounding an immediate occasion is all the baggage (positive and negative) of other weddings, funerals, ordinations, or baptisms that participants bring along with them to the ceremony. Such histories should not be spoken *about* or *at* on such occasions, but neither can they be preached *around*. The single event is the tip of an iceberg. On the other hand, no one has much interest in celebrating yet one more anniversary—even one like Christmas or Thanksgiving— unless there is a prospect of encountering something fresh and new to add to the treasures already stored in the chest of tradition.

There are other problems with making this distinction. An ordination is not just somebody's special day. Ordinations, like baptisms, are single events, but both rituals connect their participants with countless others across the ages who have been similarly called and marked. Are we celebrating a single event or a recurring observance here? The answer, clearly, is Yes!

Memorial Day and Christmas, to pose a further problem, are both occasions of celebration throughout society. But the faith-centered character of Christmas seems to put it in a quite different place homiletically than Memorial Day. So there are marked differences among the various observances we celebrate as well.

∾ Celebrations of Individuals, Religious Communities, and Cultures

Analogous challenges arise in preaching at weddings, funerals, ordinations, baptisms, and saint's days. These are all occasions celebrating individual life transitions, or focusing attention on a particular human life. The greater the preacher's sensitivity to distinctive individual dynamics on such occasions, the more effective the sermon is likely to be. It is, after all, *this* wedding, *this* ordination, *this* saint we are celebrating. Preaching on such occasions should explicitly take into account the lives of those most immediately concerned.

Easter, Christmas, Ash Wednesday, Good Friday, and Pentecost, on the other hand, are clearly church days—days that define the life of the Christian community as a whole. A highly individual focus on such occasions seriously narrows religious vision. Celebrations of Christ's incarnation, death, and resurrection can easily be sentimentalized if these feasts are not treated as the expressions of God's redeeming action in the entire sacred community.

Something similar can be said about Memorial Day, Labor Day, Thanksgiving, and Independence Day. Like Christmas and Easter, these are days for corporate focus even though the primary community is not the faith community. So it is helpful to differentiate cultural celebrations from church celebrations, and both from individual celebrations.

This framework for special occasion sermons has merit, but even so there are personal dimensions that cry out to be addressed at all community celebrations, especially Christmas and Easter. The same is true for many people on Memorial Day. On the other hand, it is inappropriate to treat a wedding, funeral, baptism, or ordination as though it were for or about the most interested parties only. A communal celebration upon such occasions is essential. And to treat the celebration of a saint in isolation from the communion of which he or she is a part is to subvert the very notion of Christian sainthood: it turns a saint into a hero.

Nor should we erect too sturdy a fence between sacred and secular holidays. Profoundly religious connotations surround Memorial Day, and there are thoroughly secular dimensions to our celebration of Christmas. Some of these may be unhealthy, but the preacher must take them into account. To do so is part of what it means to meet people where they are. Of course there is a danger in sacralizing the secular order, just as there is danger in allowing the sacred to become secular. Yet these dangers cannot be avoided by making a simple dichotomy. There is much counterfeit spirituality in our celebrations of both Christmas and Memorial Day that cannot be ameliorated by sending each feast into its own homiletical ghetto.

༝ *A Framework for Special Occasions*
So, there is both promise and peril in differentiating special occasions simply as greater or lesser feasts, as joyful, somber, or emotionally neutral situations, as one-time events or recurring observances, and as individual, religious community, or cultural celebrations. These categories clarify the homiletical

objective in some respects, but at the risk of blurring it in others. This is likely to be the case with any categories we devise.

Maybe the underlying difficulty here is that the very notion of categories tends to imply fixed boundaries marking off separate territories. There is, surely, a clear difference between preaching at an ordination and preaching on Ash Wednesday. The preacher who treats the feast of Saint Andrew as no different from the Fourth of July is making a serious mistake. Yet distinctions need not be cut and dried. They can indicate junctures, points of interplay, distinctive but mutually influencing factors.

Clearly differentiating the roles that people play in an organization, for instance, does not have to disconnect them from each other. On the contrary, the better I clearly understand my own task in the organizational scheme, the more likely it is that I will be able to help other people do their jobs without getting in their way, and to accept the assistance I need from them as well. Maybe something like that happens in a well-organized occasional sermon. Or, to return to the prism image of the last chapter, perhaps each of the variables I have called a category is actually one facet in a prism. Each refracts the light of grace in its own way, but also in its sparkling interplay with every other facet.

How do these various ways of speaking illuminate the task of preaching on a special occasion? The marking of any special occasion by a community usually involves a focus on all of the following dimensions:

- a particular person or group;
- a particular day or period of days;
- a particular event, issue, or set of circumstances.

In any given celebration, however, each of these factors will be differently proportioned or configured in relation to the others. One of these dimensions is likely to dominate any special occasion sermon, while the others inform and support it. So it is important for the preacher to know which is which, and to pay attention to the ways that the other two sets of elements can be integrated or orchestrated, in order to give the sermon richness, resonance, and complexity.

With these suggestions in mind, I propose the following framework for understanding the different kinds of special occasion preaching:

- ∾ Sermons giving particular attention to *individuals.* These include:

    —weddings and funerals, where we preach grace through individual life transitions.

    —baptisms, ordinations, and new ministry celebrations, where we preach grace through various vocations in the community of faith.

    —red-letter days and lesser feasts, where we preach grace through the lives of saints.

- ∾ Sermons giving particular attention to *days.* These include:

    —Ash Wednesday, Palm Sunday, and the Triduum of Holy Week, where we preach grace through liturgies for high holy days.

    —Christmas, Epiphany, Easter, and Pentecost, where we preach grace through festival celebrations.

    —Thanksgiving, Mother's Day, and days of special recognition, where we preach grace through civic holidays.

- ∾ Sermons giving particular attention to *circumstances.* These include:

    —social issues, theological conflicts, and crisis situations, where we preach grace through troubled waters.

—weekday homilies, guest appearances, and distinctive congregations, where we preach grace through special homiletical conditions.

—retreats, preaching missions, and liturgical seasons, where we preach grace through clearly definable periods, or episodes in the faith journey of a community.

As I have said before, such divisions are not absolute. Christmas and Easter sermons *are* about an individual person—Jesus Christ. This person, however, is of such significance for the Christian community that our celebration of his birth or the yearly remembrance of his death and resurrection cannot be treated simply as an anniversary. Each day is the liturgical mark point for one dimension of his humanity/divinity that distinctively shapes Christian identity. The church has adopted a rhythm in which different events in the life of Christ are given days of their own; hence the emphasis on the *day* rather than the *person* for sermons upon these high occasions, as well as in the Triduum of Holy Week and other dominical feasts. Moreover, the sermons included in the third group may not sound as much like special occasion sermons as they do everyday sermons artificially decked out. There is, however, a quality of the "self-contained" and the "set apart" characterizing these preaching projects that makes them worth considering in the framework of special occasion preaching.

If special occasion sermons are to be "grace-catchers," their different facets have to be specifically focused. All prisms presuppose similar principles in science and in art, but each prism exhibits these principles in distinctive ways. Effective special occasion sermons, I think, are all shaped in accordance with the basic principle we described in the last chapter: they preach not *around, about,* or *at,* but *through* the occasion. The particular demands of sermons for individual people, designated days, and significant circumstances are such, however, that we will now need to consider the patterns especially appropriate to each of these types of preaching.

PART II

Individuals as Preaching Prisms

CHAPTER FOUR

Weddings and Funerals

Preaching Grace through Rites of Passage

" It isn't the same when it's happening to you." There are many mark points that people share in common—births, deaths, weddings, graduations, job or career changes, moves from place to place. The dynamics surrounding these major transitions are familiar, even somewhat predictable. Knowing about them, however, is not the same as living through them. The obstetrician may attend the births of hundreds of babies. She may be a recognized authority in her profession, with a reputation for sensitivity and compassion. When she takes her place on the delivery table, however, it isn't the same.

What "isn't the same" is more than the obvious difference between observer and participant. There are no textbook cases of life transition—at least not to the discerning eye. The circumstances always vary from birth to birth, from one marriage to another, from one death to another. People bear witness both to their common heritage and to what makes them unique during occasions such as these. Therein lies the challenge and the opportunity: all weddings (and funerals) are the same—and no two are ever alike. Sermons in such settings need to orchestrate both the *shared* and the *singular* in the lives of those who are poised at these significant points in their lives.

The focus of this chapter is the obvious place to begin in considering different kinds of occasional service preaching. If you ask any preacher what special occasion sermons she or he most often preaches, the immediate response will probably be: "weddings and funerals." Although these two mark points seem to be at opposite ends of the spectrum, they share some similar dynamics as well. Both signal significant endings and new beginnings. Both are raw and tender times. The tears that flow on both occasions are a sign of many feelings—feelings as mixed as they are deep. How do we begin the task of celebrating in community the distinctive grace of very personal, in some ways very private, occasions? And how do the themes introduced earlier illuminate the preaching pitfalls and possibilities at weddings and funerals?

♋ Preaching Around

It used to be standard practice in many churches not to preach at either weddings or funerals. (In some places that is still the case.) Why not? Perhaps the assumption was (or is) that nothing a preacher says has any chance of being heard amidst the emotional intensity of these moments. Others have believed that because these occasions are *so* personal, grace can better be mediated solely through the time-honored words of the traditional service. Advice or admonition to the blissful or the bereaved? Theological information for the company assembled? Firm support at a fragile time of sorrow and/or joy? If any of this is to register at all, or to have any impact over the weeks and months that follow, perhaps it should be tendered through the liturgy alone.

Those who hold this point of view will readily concede that nothing the officiant recites may seem to connect with the parties concerned. Yet there is nevertheless a deep resonance between the cadences of appointed prayers and scripture passages and the hopes and fears buried in the unconscious memories of those who have come church caught up in grief or joy. Such a connection is likely to be more substantial than any bridge built by a clever or erudite sermon that showcases the personalities of the participants or their situations. A preoccupation with the uniquely personal, the argument runs, might well obscure any sense of the presence of the one Person who can really make a difference.

To eulogize the dearly departed is deadly. To give the marrying couple last-minute advice at the altar is as out of place as it is embarrassing. Better to say nothing at all! A case can certainly be made for homiletical avoidance, for leaving the situation untouched by a sermon—and yet, the cost of avoidance is high.

"Does anyone care that my mother has died? Does anyone know what it means to us that my son is getting married? Is there a word from the Lord for us, here and now?" Such questions are inevitable if the wedding or funeral rite involves nothing more than words printed on the pages of a Bible or a prayer book. If the church is a sacred community, then what it offers its members and guests at these critical points must be more than the prerecorded music at a wayside wedding chapel or the local outlet of a mortuary chain. It is primarily in the sermon that those gathered will be pointed toward the mercy of God that is *newly* present on this particular day. We *do* need to preach on the occasions of weddings and funerals. And we need to do more in our preaching than skate around the edges of the issues—which, in fact, will be a considerable temptation.

Sex and death, intimacy and mortality are topics about which our culture is squeamish. Death is denied and sex is exploited, so it is difficult to get a serious conversation started either about intimacy or mortality. Little wonder, then, that if one does hear preaching at weddings or funerals, it often sounds false and platitudinous—the equivalent of a sentimental greeting card. A sensitive handling of feelings is required in these preaching contexts, surely, but sensitivity and sentimentality are not synonymous.

The strong emotions that heavily charge these special days must be honored. They can be honored best, however, if they are allowed to flavor the sermons, rather than to serve as the primary focus. Wedding and funeral preaching are not times for complex analysis, but they are times when vividly pictured theological truths can register deeply. There is a kind of yearning vulnerability in the air upon these occasions that seldom surfaces at other times. Weddings and funerals, then, are not times to back away from addressing matters of life and death directly. That is precisely what these occasions are about.

❧ *Preaching About*

Yet those who do engage these matters of life and death often treat the occasion as though it were primarily an information session. They discharge their homiletical obligation by preaching *about* the wedding or funeral: about the beauty of intimate relationships, about the difficulties of commitment, about how Jesus "honored this manner of life by his presence and first miracle at a wedding in Galilee," about the sad inevitability of death, about the sure and certain blessed hope of resurrection, about how Jesus wept at the death of Lazarus but in the end raised him to life, all the same.

The "about" strategy certainly seems an improvement over avoidance or superficial sentimentality, but it is not necessarily so. Sentimentality at least takes immediate feelings seriously, while homiletical silence at least provides an opportunity for those rejoicing or grieving to fill in the ritual spaces themselves, connecting privately with timeless words of assurance and hope. Preaching *about* "the wedding" or "the funeral," however, can clutter up that space with abstractions and generalizations.

We seldom feel less personally engaged than when the truths of our situation are packaged for us in a box that, regardless of how professionally it is wrapped, still bears a tag marked "To Whom It May Concern." The question, again, will surely be: "But what is in it for *me?* Where do *I* fit in the picture?" Sermons delivering theological abstractions about weddings and funerals, life and death, may well intend to ground the joy and grief of the particular day in the universal grace of the gospel. Unfortunately, however, what is heard often sounds generic rather than universal.

∽ *Preaching At*

This is exactly the mistake that preaching *at* the situation does not make. This kind of wedding or funeral sermon is nothing if not particular—up close and personal: anecdotes about the couple, a *curriculum vita* of the moral virtues of the deceased, admonitions to the couple to get serious about the sacrifices of marriage and to the assembled mourners to get on with the grief process (or even, in the face of their own mortality, to "get right with God").

At first appearance, such admonitions seem to be more on target than abstract or sentimental generalizations. But the target itself is out of place. There is a profound need at weddings and funerals for words fitly spoken, but such words cannot be "in your face," however well-intended or gentle. What is right for a setting of private counseling or intimate conversation is seriously misplaced in the context of a public liturgy. It is hard enough for most of us to listen when someone undertakes to tell us what we ought to do; it is all but impossible if we realize that the advice is being overheard.

How can we preach about what marriages (or deaths) have in common, without turning the sermon into an abstraction? How can we preach to the unique circumstances of joy, grief, hope, and fear that pulse through every wedding or funeral without preaching *at* the parties so deeply affected? By preaching *through* the circumstances of these life transition points.

∾ Preaching Through

Preaching *through* an occasion means two things: honoring the *life process* of which the mark point is a symbol, and using the mark point as a *lens* through which to see a particular aspect of the grace of God. How might this be done in the context of preaching at a wedding or a funeral?

First, a sense of the day's grief or celebration will be not so much *acknowledged* as *incorporated* into the sermon. There will be an informing momentum, a pacing, a plotting of the sermon that resonates with the process of mourning or of joy. These life processes cannot, of course, be captured or contained within a sermon; they will extend over weeks, months, years. The sermon can, however, shape them *symbolically*. It can mark the time. The conflicting feelings at these events will not be subjected to psychological description or analysis, but they will be given hospitable sermon space. The classic African-American sermon does not summarize the spiritual journey of the listeners from bondage to freedom; the sermon itself takes the journey. The effective wedding or funeral sermon will make a similar journey by following the distinctive shape of the experience it addresses.

First, it is seldom necessary to "tell the story" of a couple's courtship or to recount the details of someone's battle with disease. Attention to the flow of personal circumstances, however, will almost always yield a vivid image, a rich metaphor, or an illuminating anecdote that captures a sense of the life and the transition. This the preacher can employ as a sermon lens.

Second, instead of applying scripture texts to the situation like Post-it notes, or illustrating it with personal anecdotes, the preacher is called to interpret the scripture and the situation in the light of each other. To preach *through* at the wedding or the funeral of a specific person is to find the deep connections between the movement of the scripture and the life of the person. Because this wedding or funeral is unique, it provides a unique opportunity to take a fresh look at the scriptures for a facet of grace that may have escaped our notice. ("Look at that, would you! I never saw the text in that light before!") And, of course, the illumination can work in both directions. How, the preacher will ask, do the timeless, universal truths of God's revelation help us celebrate the wedding of this fifty-year-old couple (the first time for both)? How do they help us bury that young child killed by the speeding car of a senseless drunk with a hope that is "sure and certain" because we are experiencing it as fresh and distinctive? Paradoxical though it may sound, if a preacher approaches *this* celebration with ears and eyes attuned, the points of connection will make themselves known. The listeners will feel, know, be marked by the sermon—and through it be reoriented as they move into God's future for them.

What about other transitions, such as graduation, a retirement, a move to a distant city, the undertaking of a new job, the onset of an illness, or the experience of a healing? All of these, and many more besides, can be approached in analogous fashion.

Do you remember particular sermons that have been effective in preaching *through* weddings, funerals, and other significant occasions? As I scroll through my mental file of sermons, I recall a number that were effective in the context of their respective rites of passage:

- A reaffirmation of wedding vows for a couple on the fiftieth anniversary of their marriage. The sermon for the occasion drew from the Sermon on the Mount: how those who hear and act upon the words of Jesus are like those who have built their house upon a rock.

- A memorial service for the stillborn child of artist parents. The preacher spoke of the suffering and the dying that is always involved in the artistic process, and of a suffering Christ who promises, "Behold, I am making all things new."

- A wedding for a couple, both of whom were priests. The preacher used the story of Jesus' turning water into wine at the wedding in Cana. The grace of God in the sacrament of their marriage, the preacher suggested, might be as well or better symbolized by the informal communion of the wedding reception than by the formal solemnizing of the liturgy.

- A funeral for a gospel music singer whose faith was constantly threatened by a condition of congestive heart failure. The preacher interwove the singer's struggle to believe with the story of Job, bringing both stories to sharp focus with familiar phrases: "I know that my Redeemer lives," and "I will cling to the old rugged cross."

- A marriage service for a couple deeply committed to each other yet worried (in the face of divorce statistics) about whether they would be able to maintain their vows in the face of circumstances they could not anticipate. The preacher, using the same "miracle at

Cana" story from John's gospel, spoke of Jesus as one who, in his gifts to those who marry, always "saves the best for last."

I also remember a memorial service for a young woman with a history of mental illness. One day she disappeared from her community, and though she was eventually presumed dead, her body was never found. The preacher offered consolation and closure by speaking through Jesus' words of reassurance in John 14: "Do not let your heart be troubled. Believe in God, believe also in me. In my Father's house there are many dwelling places." The sermon came to an end in the following way.

We remember that these words of our Lord were spoken at a time when death was very present. He spoke them to the cross and against the cross. He spoke them to his death and against his death, so that all might go with him through death into life eternal. And so we believe that Word. We believe that in our Father's house there are dwelling places enough for Robin, enough for us all. Because, in God's wonderful wisdom, God has chosen to speak a Word to someone who heard little of kind words. In God's gracious goodness, God has chosen to give a dwelling place to someone who for so long knew no home.

For the construction of any particular sermon, of course, no inflexible rules can be laid down. In light of what we have said thus far, however, it may be possible to suggest some homiletical rules of thumb for preaching at personal rites of passage—sermon tactics that preachers should try to avoid, and try to include.

∾ *At Weddings*

Try to avoid:

- ∾ giving advice or admonition to the couple, or to the family and friends who have gathered to wish the newly married well;
- ∾ praising the glories of married love or bewailing the divorce rate in our culture;
- ∾ drawing a heavy-handed theological connection between marriage and the church, since it has been affirmed already in the liturgy and, when badly handled, can be painful to those in the church who are not married;
- ∾ telling personal stories about this or other couples unless it is absolutely clear that they illuminate a dimension of grace in the scripture of the day.

Try to include:

- ∾ conveying a sense of the uniqueness of the individuals who are entering this particular marriage;
- ∾ celebrating the grace of God in the joys and strains of marriage;
- ∾ assuring the couple, without targeting them, of the real but nonintrusive support of those present, and of the church;
- ∾ exploring ways in which this marriage bears a *particular* witness to the grace of God.

∾ *At Funerals*

Try to avoid:

- ∾ making simplistic, upbeat assertions about resurrection and eternal life;
- ∾ extolling the virtues (real or fictitious) of the one who has died;

- ∾ "solving" the paradoxes of evil and death, or dismissing them simply as "mystery";
- ∾ imposing, or ignoring, the invitation of the gospel to those present;
- ∾ detaching oneself completely from the family's grief, or becoming utterly immersed in it.

Try to include:
- ∾ showing sensitivity to the particular circumstances of the life and death that is being celebrated and mourned;
- ∾ giving thanks for the grace manifested in the life of the one who has died;
- ∾ helping the process of expressing grief by posing questions, exploring mystery, and finding consolation;
- ∾ evoking a sense of community solidarity in the healing journey;
- ∾ setting the particular loss in a context of realistic hope by presenting the inextricable link between resurrection power and shared suffering;
- ∾ providing clear and focused references from scripture for the journey toward comfort.

CHAPTER FIVE

Baptisms, Ordinations, and Celebrations of New Ministry

Preaching Grace through Christian Vocation

"I'm really happy for her," he said. "All these years she's been doing things for her family. It's high time she got to do a little something for herself." My friend and I were talking about a woman who had just been ordained a priest. She had worked long and hard, and her efforts deserved recognition. Yet what my friend said left me feeling uneasy. Although it would have been ungracious to blurt it out then and there, when he said "a little something for herself" a voice within me protested: "That's not what ordination is about." As an observer of the ordination process from several vantage points over many years, however, I suspect that my friend's comment aptly summarizes a widely shared sense of what is going on at an ordination: it is a big liturgical "do" that is a "little something" for the ordinand.

The memory of that conversation sparks another: an all but empty church on a quiet, cold Sunday afternoon, a little family entering, well-dressed but looking frazzled, obviously ill at ease in an unfamiliar setting. They were carrying a tiny bundle—a newborn son whom they had brought for baptism in a private ceremony. The affable priest (also a friend of mine) greeted them kindly, and moved at once to make them feel more comfortable. "Why don't we all sit down here by the font and talk about how you'd like to do this," he said benignly. "After all, this is *your show.*"

Both my friends were in touch with an important truth. There is an appropriately personal focus in baptisms and ordinations, confirmations and celebrations of new ministry. That is not, however, the whole truth we need to proclaim in sermons on those days. All of these occasions seem at first to resemble weddings and funerals. In all of them, attention is focused on particular individuals who are prominently positioned at the front of the church, facing the officiating ministers. (At a funeral, the person who has died is decidedly "front and center," even if the casket or the urn with ashes is not present.) Clustered around are family members and close friends. Somewhat further back, in ordered ranks, sit those who have gathered to offer liturgical affirmation and emotional support.

These striking visual parallels, however, can be seriously misleading. Weddings and funerals are services in which the communal upholding of individuals at tender, intimate times is of primary concern. In baptisms, ordinations, confirmations, and celebrations of new ministry, however, the focus is much different. Those being baptized, ordained, confirmed, or installed are not so much the *focal point* of the service as they are its *point of departure.* Like icons in religious meditation, the candidates are a stimulus for attention and reflection, but not a terminus. Attention is appropriately directed to them only insofar as it then moves *through* and *beyond* them.

The personal attention properly given to the candidates is not intimate, private, or narrowly individual. The life of the covenant community itself is the primary focus of celebration on each of these days, even though that celebration is occasioned by a sacred rite of passage for the person at the front. Simply and bluntly put: neither the liturgy nor the sermon is "their show."

In chapter three I proposed a framework of different special occasion sermons based on the interplay of persons, days, and circumstances. That framework may be helpful here. Weddings, funerals, ordinations, baptisms, installations—all of these are special occasions on which the sermon gives particular attention to individuals. The background considerations, however—specifically, the circumstances—make a difference in the kind of homiletical attention that is appropriate for the occasion. It is God's action *in community* that sets the tone in baptisms, confirmations, ordinations, and new ministry celebrations, not the personal circumstances of the parties primarily involved.

This fact is readily apparent in the different ways that the respective events are scheduled. Days for weddings and memorial services are set primarily in accordance with the needs and wishes of family members. Scheduling conflicts may have to be negotiated between the minister and the couple seeking marriage, but no responsible minister would dream of trying to dictate the day on which a couple should tie the knot! Ordinations, confirmations, and celebrations of new ministry, on the other hand (as candidates often discover, to their frustration) are fixed, either by church policy, or in accordance with the schedule of the bishop or presiding minister. Baptisms (if they are celebrated in accordance with ancient practice) are administered on Easter, Pentecost, the feast of All Saints, or the Baptism of Our Lord—designated calendar days that are held in common by the entire church. The protocols in all these cases are not arbitrary conventions; they indicate something significant about the particular center of attention that is integral to the different occasions.

As we did in the last chapter, let's see what might be involved in preaching *around, about, at,* and *through* these occasions—occasions in which the primary facet of grace is community vocation.

ᕕ *Preaching Around*

Since baptisms, confirmations, ordinations, and celebrations of new ministry almost always have special orders of service appointed for the day, it is unlikely that preachers will be tempted to preach *around* these occasions in the sense of avoiding them altogether. Instances of the homiletical "red herrings" we talked about in chapter two are rampant, however; preaching on these occasions often fails to get to the heart of the matter. All of these special occasions, unfortunately, are fertile breeding grounds for sentimentality at the expense of substance.

Such sentimentality often results when the sermons get stuck in a narrowly personal focus. Baptisms, confirmations, ordinations, and celebrations of new ministry are often treated as if they were religious graduation or award ceremonies. They are not. We do not need to hear nice words about what a happy day this is; how proud the parents must be; how honorable is the estate to which the candidate has been called. Nor do we need to hear a lecture about the baptismal covenant, the doctrine of the church, the nature of the vocational diaconate, or the liturgical functions reserved to the presbyterate. What we *do* need to hear on these occasions is God's clear, strong word to the church.

∾ Preaching About

A bit of reflection, a little imagination, and a bumper crop of unpleasant sermon memories will probably be all you need in order to make relevant application to the "community vocation" preaching that is the subject here. Preaching *about* such occasions includes:

- ∾ erudite treatises on the early history of Christian baptism;
- ∾ detailed discussions of the respective roles of the four orders of ministry ("as found in the Catechism which appears on page 855 of the *Book of Common Prayer*—will everyone please pick up a prayer book and turn to that page?");
- ∾ simple reiteration of parts of the special liturgy ("As the newly installed minister will shortly pray: 'O Lord God, I am not worthy to have you come under my roof'");
- ∾ commentaries on the significance of what the congregation is "really saying" in the prayers for the candidates, the liturgy for ordinations, the welcoming of the newly baptized, or the symbolic giving of gifts to the newly installed minister.

Small wonder that such sermons seldom spark any celebration!

Lest this sound unduly dismissive, let me quickly acknowledge that the church is not likely to thrive unless it is deeply grounded in a rich understanding of ecclesiology—of what it means, before and within God, to be *church*. Systematic analyses or scattered sentiments that are saved up for and dumped off on these occasions, however, do not produce the needed effect. Nor do sermons that trail off into reminiscences.

- ∾ "Remember how it was in the fifties, when everyone came to church?"

ᰍ "The noble sacrifices of these faithful stalwarts inspire
us today."

ᰍ "How vividly I recall the day on which I was ordained."

Nor, again, do sermons that are lectures on:

ᰍ the state of the church at the end of Christendom;

ᰍ the inescapable challenge of religious pluralism;

ᰍ the new millennium;

ᰍ the new kinds of ministry demanded by different
cultural paradigms.

Such sermons are not rich in their ecclesiology. All of them
are a far cry from a perceptive description of what *God* has
done, is doing, and promises to do in establishing the reign of
everlasting righteousness for which all creatures long—which
is both cause for celebration, and a celebration in itself. Such a
celebration is engaging in a way that dispensing information
can never be.

ᰍ *Preaching At*

If preaching *about* the church, its members, or its ministries
tends to wear thin, what about something more direct? A
sermon "to" *(at)* the candidate or the congregation may seem
a more attractive option than an information session.

ᰍ "And now, will the ordinands please rise to receive
their charge?"

ᰍ "These parents cannot possibly bring up this child
unless you, the congregation, hold them accountable,
which means that *you too* are accountable."

ᰍ "All too often, once the ceremony is over, the
confirmands are out the door of the church for good.
God grant, my dear young people, that this will not be
so of you."

ᰍ "The new pastor of this parish will only be as effective
as the people of this parish are faithful."

Such homiletical devices seem fitting to many preachers; otherwise their listeners would not have to suffer through so many of them. The question is, however (even if somewhat crassly put): how is the sanctuary being used in a way that is all that different from a high school football locker room at half-time when the team is down six points? A bully pulpit is no more appropriate on these occasions than a lecture podium.

To place candidates or congregations in the seat of honor on one of these occasions may be better than putting them on the hot seat. But the compliments and congratulations so often dispensed in these sermon are roughly analogous to eulogies at funerals and humorous anecdotes about the couple that serve as substitutes for wedding homilies. The problem, of course, is that either positive or negative focus on the central human figures in any of these rites—especially in rites of ministry celebration—unintentionally shifts them from *icons* to *idols*. What everyone is there to celebrate is not *my* ministry, *our* ministry, *their* ministry—but the ministry of *Christ* to his Body, and through his Body to the world. How can the sermon be a grace-catcher of *that* light in these celebrations of community vocation?

ꙮ *Preaching Through*
What is the alternative to compliments, injunctions, and information? What is the heart of the matter that these sermon strategies, even if misfocused, are earnestly desiring to touch? How can the deep hunger of these occasions be connected with the mighty acts of God? How do we make God's story of salvation fresh and illuminating for this particular mark point in the church's life? How do we prevent that story from sounding like a graduation speech? By selecting and employing specific aspects of salvation history

as the sermon *melody,* while orchestrating cultural, personal, theological, and liturgical materials in relation to that theme. The melody line of a piece of music, if sung or played alone, can eventually begin to sound trite. A melody line must be simple in order to be memorable, yet any tune, however catchy, can sound trivial after a while. If all I had ever heard of Dvorak's *New World Symphony* was a single note version of its "Going Home" theme, I might well conclude that this symphony was not such an impressive piece of music. What makes Dvorak a musical genius is not his use of melody lines, but his orchestral imagination: the myriad ways that the fundamental themes he employs are harmonically engaged and underscored. But all the different shades of his harmonizations would be lost on the listener if they were not woven through the melody lines and through each other as they develop the symphony's main themes.

"God calls us—both individually and corporately—into covenant community, envelopes and empowers us in unconditional love, and sends us forth to proclaim good news to the poor, release to captives, and recovery of sight to the blind." What else is there to say in sermons at baptisms, confirmations, ordinations, and new ministry celebrations? Nothing—and everything. The problem with many sermons on such occasions is that they either reduce the richness of that theme to a single melody line or they try to improve upon the familiar and obvious by informing, exhorting, or complimenting the candidates.

But what if the sermon had as its center one particular scene or aspect of the drama of salvation, such as:

- ∾ the baptism of Jesus, followed by his temptation;
- ∾ the annunciation to Mary, the song of Hannah;
- ∾ the call of Moses, Isaiah, or Jeremiah;
- ∾ the pastoral struggles of St. Paul with the arrogant spirituality of the church in Corinth, the legalisms of

the Galatians, or the eschatological anxiety of the Christians in Thessalonica;

∾ Jesus' response to conditions that threaten the life of a vulnerable community ("Behold, I am sending you out like sheep in the midst of wolves"; "The greatest among you must be like the youngest");

∾ the prophetic vision of a field of dry bones, or of a feast of fat things on the mountain of the Lord;

∾ the imperative "feed my sheep" to one who had reason to think he would never again be trusted.

Suppose the sermon took one of these as its source? (Which does not necessarily mean starting the sermon with it, or dwelling on it for most of the sermon.) What if the preacher found connections between the chosen text of scripture and the individual circumstances of the candidate, ordinand, or new minister, with the poetics of the liturgy, or with issues in the church that seem especially pressing? If scripture and situation were heard *through* each other, and developed much as a musical theme is developed, that sermon just might spark a celebration!

If you glance quickly at all the scriptural stories and situations listed above, I think you can probably agree that all of them have something to do with God's empowering call to ministry. Some of these biblical passages even share significant features (a call narrative, a prophetic oracle, a healing story, a "saying" of Jesus). Yet the common melodic theme does not become boring through its repetition because in these different scripture texts we hear the melody through many variations and experience it as rich and engaging. Repetition only increases our interest, stimulating questions, insights, and a sense of personal connection.

Sermons at baptisms, confirmations, ordinations, and new ministry celebrations could hardly do better. The task is not simply to replay the scripture in the sermon, but to let the drama of scripture serve as a model for, and a stimulus to, the exploring of tensions, traumas, and graces that we encounter in our own adventures of Christian vocation.

What might such a sermon look like? Let's look at a couple of examples. The first is a baptismal sermon, set in the context of an Easter Vigil. The preacher begins:

> If you are like me, you probably enjoy stories. The stories we read and the stories we tell say who we are. Stories give us our name. And our name is our story. One of my favorite stories is *The Lord of the Rings.* Do you know it? I am sure you do. In *The Lord of the Rings* one finds out very early on that stories tell the names of things.

The preacher quickly sketches the setting and major characters of J. R. R. Tolkien's classic trilogy about "Middle Earth," and then turns to a scene where the hobbits, Merry and Pippin, encounter an Ent—a talking tree.

> Merry and Pippin ask the Ent his name. Listen to what the Ent has to say in reply:

> > I am not going to tell you my name; not yet, at any rate. For one thing, it would take a long while. My name is growing all the time, and I've lived a very long, long time; so my name is like a story. Real names tell you the story of things they belong to in my language.

> This night, in the lovely language of the Easter Vigil, we have told our name, and it is a very long, long name. For our name is not only in the present. Our name reaches back before the dawn of time. And our name reaches into the future beyond time. Woven into our names are many other names, and each of our names has a story.

The preacher then proceeds to recount the story of creation in Genesis, the Exodus story of Israel's deliverance at the Red Sea, and Ezekiel's vision of new life in the valley of dry bones.

These stories, and many more besides which are woven within them, tell our name. In the Exsultet, that wonderful poem of light which we sing at the beginning of the Vigil, we set the focus of our story, the Paschal Mystery. The Paschal Mystery is the core of our name. The Paschal Mystery is that Christ paid the price for Adam's sin. And by his blood, Christ delivered God's faithful people. In the Exsultet, the story of the past is brought into sharp focus in the present. Not a night five, or ten, or fifteen thousand years ago. But *this* night is the night when God brought our forebears out of bondage. *This* is the night when all who believe in Christ are delivered from sin and restored to grace. How blessed is this night! And how blessed is this, our name!

This night, in churches round the world, many people, young and old, will be baptized. For many others, baptismal vows will be renewed. In baptism we not only give names, but take names unto ourselves as well. Through baptisms, new names are grafted onto our name. And so the story continues. Our name is growing all the time.

In Christ's name is our name. Through his name, Christ has grafted us onto his story. And his story is the story of life. Real names tell you the story of the things they belong to. And we belong to Christ; that is our name. This night, when you leave this place, go tell our name, so that for generations to come, people will know who we are, and want to weave their stories into our story, and make their name our name, for that is the baptismal meaning of this Vigil. Our name is Christ's name. It is a long name. And it takes a long time to tell.

Here Tolkein's Ent provides a fresh way of approaching both the lessons appointed for the Vigil, and the Exsultet. The scriptures and the liturgical hymn are used in the sermon but not subjected to analysis. We move through the historical drama of God's covenant love into the baptismal covenant; we do not refer to, discuss, or simply "think about" these passages, but experience them firsthand. We are invited, at the sermon's end, to "go tell our name." And yet (as I can attest, being among those in whose presence this sermon was preached) the listeners are not being ordered or exhorted. By the time the preacher has brought us to this point, he is naming aloud for and with us what all of us are yearning to do. The preacher at this primal liturgy of baptism has preached *through* the occasion.

It is possible for the personalities of the candidates being marked for Christian vocation to figure somewhat more prominently in the sermon without necessarily stealing the show. The following is a sermon for the ordination to the priesthood of a woman who has an active clown ministry with her youth group, who served as ushers at her ordination dressed in full costume. With special dispensation from the ordaining bishop (since the text was not among those appointed for ordination), the second reading is 1 Corinthians 1:17-25, where Paul declares that "God's foolishness is wiser than human wisdom."

The preacher begins by inviting listeners to imagine a time when they had been excited by a great idea, only to be told "Don't be a fool!" "Nobody likes to be called a fool," the preacher observes,

> which makes St. Paul kind of hard to figure, doesn't it?
> Paul doesn't mind in the least being considered a fool.
> He's even willing to call *God* a fool as well. Paul goes on
> and on about the foolishness of God. It's a wonder God
> didn't pick up a thunderbolt and nuke St. Paul right on

the spot. It is also a wonder that Paul's words about foolishness appear so prominently in this morning's ordination service. After all, who wants to talk about being a fool when one is becoming a priest?

Surely, it's festivity we are concerned about here, not foolishness. For St. Paul to prattle on about the foolishness of the gospel—it's in bad taste—like coming to a formal dinner party dressed as a clown. So—why did Patricia invite St. Paul to this party, anyway?

The preacher goes on to give some examples of God's "foolishness," drawn from the other lessons: the calling of Isaiah, and the Good Shepherd laying down his life for the sheep. This is how the sermon ends:

> What does it really mean to be a fool? The heart of the matter is this: Being a fool means holding up a vision of reality that seems just too good to be true. Leave the flock to find a single sheep? Bring other sheep into an already well-established flock—and risk all the hassle of conflict in the sheepfold, not to mention the difficulties of crowd control? That's crazy! Sheer foolishness. It doesn't compute.

> But wouldn't it be wonderful, if, all evidence to the contrary, life really did run on the kind of radically different program that Jesus proclaimed? Well, Isaiah and Jeremiah, Moses and Miriam, Mary Magdalene, and Gertrude the Great [Patricia's "matron saint"]—all of these folks, and many more, prick up their ears when they hear of such foolishness. They find the prospects so exciting that they spread the word—willing to look like fools themselves just on the chance that still other folks too might hear the message, catch the spirit, and live the truth of a God whose love will never let go.

> It is to a life of such foolishness that we ordain Patricia.

Foolishly singing God's Divine Comedy does not mean denying the world's tragedy. Look closely in the face of the clown. Do you see the clown's eyes? Often as not, they are filled with tears.

Nevertheless, with eyes wide open to the suffering of the world, Patricia will lead us to see the city of God planted and flourishing in the very center of all the world's cynicism, and despair. The foolishness of God is wiser than human wisdom. By the foolishness of Patricia's preaching, God will reduce the weary wisdom of the world to a joyful frolic of forgiveness and freedom. Like St. Paul, like Isaiah, like the Good Shepherd, and like Gertrude the Great, Patricia will be among us as a Holy Fool. It does seem too good to be true. But that isn't likely to squelch for a single second the sparkle of Patricia's priestly foolishness. Thanks be to God.

While this is a sermon for and about a particular person, it is more fundamentally a sermon about *God,* and about God's empowering call to ministry.

Can we make any summary statements about preaching at baptisms, ordinations, confirmations, and celebrations of new ministry? What should we try to avoid, and try to include?

Try to avoid:
- discussions of the state of the church;
- abstract treatments of the theology of ministry;
- compliments to the newly baptized, confirmed, ordained, or installed;
- heavy-handed exhortations to the new minister or the congregation;
- sentimentality about the trials and triumphs of ministry;
- appeals for more ministers—lay or ordained.

Try to include:

- a celebration of the ministry of Christ as the model of all ministry;
- a connection with stories from scripture that show God at work in the human struggle to discern and work out sacred vocation;
- an invitation to Christian vocation as an unfolding adventure;
- an exploration of tensions, struggles, gifts, and graces of ministry evident in this particular minister and the congregation;
- an assurance of God's presence and the promise of communal support for those who are marking a transition point in ministry.

CHAPTER SIX

Red Letter Days
and Lesser Feasts

Preaching Grace through the Lives of Saints

In one of the seminaries where I often visit there is a large dining hall with high ceilings and sky-blue walls. Along the walls, on all four sides of the room and positioned several feet above eye level, is an array of formal portraits depicting a great cloud of witnesses, all of them significant and distinguished figures in the seminary's history. The first time I walked into the room, I had the distinct impression that all of them were saying in unison to the diners far below: "Sit up straight and eat your peas!" I wondered if their gaze might have a negative impact on the digestion of those who were eating. A few more visits to the room during lunch time let me know that I had little cause for concern. Nobody seemed to pay the portraits any attention, except for the time when some students bedecked a few of the portraits, turning them temporarily into cartoons.

This lack of recognition might be a source of frustration to the donors of these portraits, but it is probably an irritant to which they have become resigned. After all, in our culture not much honor is accorded to ancestors. Statues and stained glass windows stimulate the curiosity of sightseers, but they seldom evoke the reverence of pilgrims.

Our celebration of those whom the church has designated "saints" is often similarly careless. Certain religious devotees (and church history buffs) take the communion of saints with great seriousness; some people feel personal affection for a patron saint. To many of us, however, saints are irrelevant. Those with strongly Protestant leanings frequently regard the whole subject with suspicion or even open hostility: "Jesus is my savior. I don't need any intermediaries! Lives of the saints? Legends at best! Shrines and relics? Superstitious nonsense! Prayer to the saints? Idolatry!"

If we in the church are not of a single mind about saints, it is no wonder that we do not know how to preach with them! Some preachers refuse to touch them (except insofar as they are biblical characters one might employ as convenient sermon illustrations). Others use saints' days as occasions for getting in what they regard as necessary remedial lessons in church history or theology. Still others use the lives of saints as moral object lessons: "What does St. Francis have to teach us, we who are so caught up in our attractions to worldly wealth, and so reticent to suffer with the poor for the sake of Christ?"

By this time you will doubtless recognize the pattern:

- ✤ preaching *around* the saints;
- ✤ preaching *about* the saints;
- ✤ using the saints to preach *at* the congregation.

We do not need, at this point, to retrace the general contours of this framework. Let's look at some of the ways in which the patterns manifest themselves in this preaching context.

✤ Preaching Around

Why would preachers want to avoid addressing the saints in their sermons? Because there does seem to be a certain oddness—if not a definite danger—in using a sermon to point in the direction of those who themselves constantly say, in word and action: "Don't look at me; look at the One whom I serve." The human psyche is prone to hero worship, whether our idols are film stars, athletic giants, political dignitaries, or remarkable religious personalities. No human being can bear the weight of what Paul Tillich so aptly designated "Ultimate Concern." These great individuals stand before us as larger than life, although they inevitably crack and crumble when leaned upon too heavily.

Still, most people seem to have a strong attraction to VIPs. A particular human model is more tangible and accessible than a transcendent God. And the commandment "Thou shalt have no other gods before me" has always been a precept easier to give than to obey. So why put stumbling blocks before the vulnerable? Why tempt a sermon listener so strongly at such an obvious point of human weakness? Thus reason those who regularly issue calls to holiness in their sermons but prefer to do it without reference to the saints. As evidence for their position, they can easily point to the sentimental pietism or works-righteousness moralism that often characterize sermons about the saints.

These reasons are difficult to fault. Yet we need to be connected with the stories of our whole community, past and present, in order to understand who we are and how we can effectively minister. If this is so, then it is all but impossible to live a vital Christian life without a palpable awareness of our fellow communicants—those who are living and those who have entered into joy. I cannot effectively know myself until I see myself reflected in my fellow human beings. I best discern my own vocation in seeing my similarities and my differences with others—ways in which I am graced, tempted, and challenged that are not identical, but are analogous to others.

If healthy role models and fellow companions on the journey are not available, I will inevitably find my way into poorer company. What a pity it is if the great cloud of witnesses who are available to support us in our faith journeys are never introduced! If this company remains a faceless crowd, then I will probably stumble along, blinded by the tragic and unnecessary assumption that I am running the race all by myself.

∾ *Preaching About*

"So there is a good reason for church history lessons after all! You can't know who you are if you don't know your history! Today the church remembers Perpetua and her Companions. Tradition tells us that Perpetua was a young widow, mother of an infant and owner of several slaves...." The sermon *about* is off and running—in this case, with the first line of the bibliographical information from *Lesser Feasts and Fasts*. The tragedy is that the relevant page from this resource (or its equivalent) is often presented as the sermon itself—as though historical data were self-illuminating.

The time we have spent reflecting on other sermons focusing grace through particular persons (those to be baptized, ordained, installed, married, or buried) is useful here, too. However interesting it may be to the preacher, information *about* an individual is not in itself a proclamation of the gospel. A eulogy does not function as a "grace-catcher" at a funeral. Is data from *Lesser Feasts and Fasts* essentially any different? Not if it simply gives us names and dates, facts and figures, and not if it simply recounts the exploits that have led the church to canonize this person.

❧ *Preaching At*

"Which is precisely why we must not lose the opportunity to press the point of moral connection! If Perpetua can be faithful unto death in witness to her Lord and Savior—even to the point of helping to guide the sword of her inept executioner—than surely you and I, by the grace of God...." Here the preacher fills in the blank with whatever he or she envisions will challenge the congregation without pushing them over the edge of credibility.

We *do* need role models; we *do* need inspiration. Someone who has "been there, done that" may serve as a combination moral compass and morale booster. The question is, however, whether such exhortation is effective in energizing us over the long haul—and, indeed, whether it is healthy, even if it does. It is a very serious question, I think, as to whether it is appropriate for saints to be regarded as the religious community's equivalent of secular heroes and heroines. There are similarities; but there are significant differences as well.

Heroic men and women are accorded that status because of certain *achievements,* and they remain "stars" only as long as the list of accomplishments keeps lengthening (or, in the case of a dead hero, as long as the record of accomplishments is not undermined by subsequent revelations, or the work of historical revisionists). "Look at the good things she or he *did!*"—that is the implication, followed by, "If you have a dream, work hard and make sacrifices. You might just achieve this kind of recognition as well."

The fundamental claim that our faith tradition makes about saints, however, is different. "Look at what God has done through the life of one who showed little promise as a moral athlete or a religious superstar! If God's grace can work even under *those* conditions, then surely it can transform and inspire each member of the Christian community—maybe even me—in unique and surprising ways."

"Why can't you be more like that splendid St. Swithin?" That is the clear implication in a great deal of "saint sermon" language, familiar to the ears of anyone who has been unfavorably compared, unkindly or benignly, with somebody who is presumably "better." When confronted with it in the language of preaching, the sermon listener will either shut down or resort to bursts of energy fruitlessly trying to become more "saintly." But the fact of the matter remains: few people, if any, are effectively inspired to significant achievement by being faced with the fact that someone in the next row gets higher test scores than they do.

ꙮ Preaching Through

How grace comes *through* the lives of saints—celebrated or unknown, full of achievement or dogged by constant failure—*that* is what we need to hear in sermons on red letter days and lesser feasts. How can that sense of mercy, mediated through the human condition, be itself mediated effectively through the homiletical art form?

What the preacher is searching for in the preparation of sermons for such occasions is an insight about how grace may be encountered in the struggles, joys, and sorrows of everyday existence. Seeing grace "live" in the experience of others will not give us rules to follow or make our decisions for us. It will not give us advance notice of precisely how grace can be expected to operate in our circumstances. It will give us clues, however. It will expand our horizons and sharpen our peripheral vision. It will position us to recognize and trust our own surprises of grace when they come to us.

How does that actually translate into specific sermon strategies? By shifting the homiletical focus away from information to be imparted, behavior to be encouraged, or achievements to be honored and emulated. By paying attention instead to gifts bestowed on the saint, to revelations encountered in unlikely places, and to the interplay between the appointed scriptures and the saint's own journey. By tracking with a saint's unfolding adventure in faith rather than simply tacking up purported accomplishments.

For the feast of Perpetua and her Companions, for example, readings are appointed from Hebrews 10 and Matthew 24. Both offer exhortations to persevere in the face of persecution. What is striking about these passages, however, is that each ends not with an *imperative*, but with an encouraging *indicative*. "We are not among those who shrink back and so are lost," says the author of the letter to the Hebrews (who are, in fact, facing the threat of persecution). We are, instead, "among those who have faith and so are saved" (v. 39). Matthew's Jesus tells his disciples, in the context of an apocalyptic discourse: "This good news of the kingdom will be proclaimed throughout the world, as a testimony to all nations; and then the end will come" (v. 14). A striking feature in the story of Perpetua's martyrdom is the fact that the members of the company, even as they were being tortured, called out to each other in encouragement and support. They strengthened one another's witness by adding to it. In the face of immediate suffering, they enabled each other to remain grounded in the deeper truth of God's indestructible grace. With a little imaginative connecting, *that* will preach!

What is being suggested here, obviously, is a specific application of what we discussed in chapter two: preaching *through* a special occasion involves being sensitive to movement, history, and process, while using the scripture lessons and the human situation as mutually illuminating. The tendency on saints' days is either toward *prescription*

("What do we learn here about what we ought to do?")—in other words, preaching *at*—or toward *flat description* ("X was born in the seventh century, the fourth of six children"), or preaching *about*. The more effective alternative is *imaginative description:* the search for a fresh angle of vision on what it means for us to be empowered by God, a vision that comes from seeing the text of the scripture and the life of the saint in light of one another.

Such an approach to preaching on the saints will take them off the gallery wall, or at least bring them down to eye level. Making them human does not mean muckraking—showing that they, after all, have feet of clay. Rather, such preaching makes the saints a living part of our ongoing anxieties, passions, and conversations.

One way to "honor" a dignitary is to read out a long list of awards and accomplishments. To do so, however, is to honor in the abstract. Those to whom the dignitary is thus introduced may be impressed, and they may clamor for an autograph or a photo opportunity. But how different it is when you introduce to a group of friends someone who has influenced you profoundly, someone whom you really respect! You try to find points of connection between the parties; you set out to build bridges. You are convinced that your friends will also hold this person in high regard, and will come to honor him or her as you do. Or, better yet, honor that person in ways that are unique to their own relationships.

Formal introductions are often more awkward than the associations struck up when people come together in a common activity or quest. If the saint's day sermon is modeled on the formal introduction, it is likely to produce a stiff, unnatural portrait. If the sermon in celebration of a saint is more like the more informal introduction—if we and the saint are invited to go adventuring together—then the association is likely to be both more intimate and more profound.

Thereafter, in the midst of running the race that is set before us, when we raise our eyes to the great cloud of witnesses, our eyes will make contact here and there with the eyes of friends—and we will run with renewed energy.

Once again, let's consider some examples. The first is a sermon for the feast of St. Thomas, which occurs in the last week of Advent, just before Christmas. The preacher begins by reminding us that at this time of year everything around us encourages us to suspend our belief in the hard realities before our eyes, and dream of a "white Christmas." In Advent many of the scripture lessons seem to do the same ("Every valley shall be filled, and every mountain shall be made low"), but

> the fact of the matter is: the mountains are still as tall as ever, and the number of people fearing disaster seems to be on the increase. What a relief to celebrate Thomas the Apostle—Doubting Thomas—just a few days before Christmas. At least he is honest in the face of impossible news: "Unless I put my finger in the mark of the nails and my hand in his side, I will not believe."
>
> Thomas is not interested in divine earth moving. You can leave the mountains where you like. Thomas is a literal-minded man. He was an enthusiastic disciple of Jesus, but his hopes and dreams were destroyed as he watched Jesus arrested, tried, and crucified.
>
> Thomas was a believer once, but there is no point in getting hopes up again. That would be too painful. "Give me a sign," Thomas is asking. "Let me touch the wounds of Jesus." So Jesus appears and shows him the wounds, and Thomas "meets Jesus again for the first time."
>
> For the first time, Thomas learns that Jesus is not confined by time and space. Thomas learns that the Christ cannot be confined to *his* idea of who Jesus is. It is not *Thomas* who gets to define and determine the parameters of his relationship with Jesus.

Our sense of reality is altered when we learn that following Jesus means following him in any form that he might take. Believing in Jesus does not mean suspending our belief in reality, but expanding it. Believing in Jesus means packing up our preconceived notions of who Jesus is, and leaving them behind. It means meeting Jesus in surprising and new ways: Jesus Christ is the shepherd, the king, the bread of life, the risen wounded man, a baby.

Along the Christian journey, we get to meet Jesus again and again. As the risen, wounded one, he is invincible against the injustice of the world. As a baby, he is vulnerable to that same injustice. With St. Thomas, we are not called to *suspend* the reality we see, but we are invited to *reach beyond the confines* of that reality, and to ask how Jesus is showing himself to us today.

The lens through which this sermon is focused is the conversion of Thomas. Notice how it "plays" the conversion dramatically, inviting us into emotional identification with his disbelief. Notice also how the sermon integrates the pressures of a secular holiday, the vision of Advent, the Easter event, and the Nativity of Our Lord with swift, deft strokes. The faith journey Thomas takes becomes a faith journey into which we are incorporated. And the "conclusion" of the sermon is as open-ended as was Thomas's encounter with the Risen Lord.

The second sermon is shaped for the celebration of All Saints' Day, and the primary icon is neither a "red letter" nor a "lesser" saint, but someone who could well live just around the block. The preacher begins with the familiar words of Jesus from the Beatitudes that "shake up our conception of the blessed life," and then she turns to the lesson from Ecclesiasticus, which warns that "If you serve the Lord, prepare yourself for temptation.... Gold is tested in the fire, and acceptable people in the furnace of humiliation." In the light of these lessons the preacher asks:

> Could it be that we have spent our energy looking for the saints in all the wrong places? Could it be that it is in those places that we avoid—the place of chaos, poverty, and fear, that place where things seem out of control, that furnace of humiliation—that we discover the birthplace of sainthood?
>
> If Jesus is right, then I think that we have got it all wrong. To be a saint, to be blessed, is to live and love amidst the fires of life. Fire will engulf you when you least expect it, illumining your poverty, making you see your need for God. Fires will shape you, mold you, transform you—if you are willing to be blessed.
>
> Let me tell you about one saint who saw God's goodness in the midst of the fire, and waits patiently to see more. His name is Tommy. He's nine years old. He's been on the news lately, perhaps you've seen him. His father was in a coma for seven years. Seven years of waiting, and then, one day, his father woke up. He sat up in bed and talked with his brother, with his wife, his sons. And the doctors just didn't know what to make of it all. It was beyond their understanding, beyond their control. Just as unexpectedly, about five days later, Tommy's father slipped back into the coma. Again, the doctors had no explanation. They could offer no medical reason why he had woken up and why he had slipped back.
>
> A woman from CNN interviewed Tommy and his older brother, who is eleven. Tommy's brother answered most of the questions. Yes, they were hoping that their dad would come back again and talk to them. Yes, they were sad that he had slipped back into a coma so soon, but they would wait. The interviewer kept reiterating how tragic this must have seemed to the two

boys. But Tommy could not stop smiling. Finally, the interviewer had to ask, "Why do you seem so happy?"

"Because," said the little boy, "my dad woke up and told me that he loved me."

Be patient, says Ecclesiasticus. Gold is tested in the fire, and acceptable people in the furnace of humiliation. Tommy is patient, and he sees what is important. He is willing to wait, to be tested and refined, even if it takes a lifetime.

Today we will baptize new members into the Body of Christ. We will mark two young people as Christ's own forever. With the cool waters of baptism, we will make a sign on their foreheads, reminding them of the coolness of God's hand amidst the fires of life. No, we cannot protect these children from life's difficulties, from life's pain. But we can prepare them for the heat by bathing them in living water, water which will sustain and nourish them in the heat of the day, water which signifies for us and for them that they are blessed by God.

Do you want to be a saint? Then remember your baptism and be thankful—not for a life of ease and comfort, but thankful that, by God's grace, we are daily being formed by the fires and refined into sainthood.

One of the things that is probably very apparent by now is the way in which the various facets of grace can dance together in a single sermon if each is carefully cut and polished. A baptism sermon for an Easter Vigil, a saint's day sermon that celebrates Easter and Christmas, an All Saints' Day sermon that celebrates baptism—in no case are the additional special occasion elements simply "added on." Instead, the preacher hones in sharply on the needs of a specific occasion, and then incorporates the rich secondary emphases of other occasions.

What will we be trying to avoid and to include in sermons at the celebration of a saint?

Try to avoid:

- ✑ extended biographical details, except as they relate to the plot of the sermon;
- ✑ general information about church history or theology appropriate to a lecture or a group study session, unless it has an immediate bearing on the insight the sermon is attempting to foster or evoke;
- ✑ presentation of the saint as a "hero," or simply as an "all-too-human" anti-hero ("trashing" the saints is no more helpful than idealizing them);
- ✑ moralism, comparison, and exhortation to "try to be like X."

Try to include:

- ✑ a mutual illumination of the text of scripture and the life of the saint;
- ✑ an invitation of praise and thanksgiving for the rich diversity of gifts that are manifest in the whole communion of saints;
- ✑ an awareness of the particular ways in which the grace of God is revealed through unlikely circumstances;
- ✑ a recognition that God uses experiences and idiosyncrasies that are *analogous* to (not "just like") our own.

PART III

Days as Preaching Prisms

CHAPTER SEVEN

Ash Wednesday, Palm Sunday, and the Triduum

Preaching Grace through Liturgies
for Holy Days

"We don't preach on Palm Sunday," the priest informed me matter-of-factly. "The dramatic reading of the passion gospel *is* the sermon. Nothing one might say after that could possibly add anything! Besides, with everything else going on," he said (referring to the opening festival procession), "nobody ever listens to a Palm Sunday sermon anyway."

Since I was relatively new to the Episcopal Church at the time, I had assumed that preaching on such a significant occasion would be a given. So I checked the directions for the Palm Sunday service in the *Book of Common Prayer:* "When the Liturgy of the Palms has preceded, the Nicene Creed and the Confession of Sin may be omitted at this service." No mention is made of omitting the sermon, so presumably the normal expectation of preaching at the "principal service of worship" on Sunday applies.

I shrugged my shoulders and went about my own business. Shortly thereafter I received a ruder shock. I was attending the Good Friday service at a seminary that prides itself on meticulous attention to liturgical detail. The service unfolded at great length, with rich musical offerings and all the traditional liturgical elements for the day. The passion gospel from John was movingly chanted by well-rehearsed cantors—and there was no sermon! The service proceeded immediately to the Solemn Collects and the Veneration of the Cross, both elaborately choreographed.

Again I went to the prayer book in my choir stall, and found the rubrics regarding the passion gospel. The line immediately beneath these instructions could not have been more clear: "The sermon follows." Subsequent conversation with the local liturgical authorities produced a response essentially similar to that of the Palm Sunday priest: on this day the liturgy itself is "so powerful" that anyone bold enough to preach would inevitably be standing in its way. Actions speak louder than words, so we should just let the liturgy do the talking.

Anyone who has ever had to sit through someone's earnest, tortured effort to "explain" a picture, a poem, or even a joke will appreciate such a rationale, as will anyone who has suffered through Holy Week sermons that go on and on in the midst of already vivid liturgies, thus seriously undermining their power. Only homiletical insensitivity—or outright arrogance—could disregard or compete with the rich scriptural and liturgical resources that make high holy days so different from other days.

Avoidance, however, is not the antidote: *no* preaching is not an improvement upon *poor* preaching. How, then, can one preach well upon such occasions? How can preaching effectively complement the worship patterns that are proper to these solemn celebrations? How may we preach *through* them? Sermons that operate independently of the liturgies of the day (preaching *around*), sermons that constantly draw attention either to the special rubrics, prayers, or worship patterns (preaching *about),* sermons that tell those present what they should be thinking, feeling, or doing (preaching *at)*—all such sermons are likely to altogether miss or seriously misuse a rich homiletical opportunity. When the sermon plays a well-shaped role in the larger liturgical drama of the occasion, however, worship can be "powerful" in the best sense of the word.

Five days appear in the calendar of the church year for which there are special liturgies: Ash Wednesday, Palm Sunday, Maundy Thursday, Good Friday, and the Great Vigil of Easter. Each of these five liturgical days has a very different character, so it is best to consider each in its own right. How the preacher deals with the appointed scripture lessons for these days, of course, will vary from preacher to preacher, year to year, text to text, and from one congregation to another. The drama of each of these occasions, however, does seem to be driven by a particular paradox that the liturgy picks up, and artfully underscores.

- ∾ On Ash Wednesday, we meet a God who confronts our fragile humanity with radical compassion.
- ∾ On Palm Sunday, we meet a God who displays divine power through participating in two seemingly contradictory human parades through Jerusalem.
- ∾ On Maundy Thursday, we meet a hands-on God who is washing feet one minute and breaking bread the next.
- ∾ On Good Friday, we meet a God who saves life while losing it.
- ∾ At the Great Vigil of Easter, we meet a God whose actions are at once "ancient history" and part of the here and now.

In each case, the preacher has an opportunity: not to explain the liturgy, nor to exhort gathered listeners to live up to "the moral of the story," but to shape a *homiletical* celebration that complements the *liturgical* celebration.

The possibilities for imaginative preaching *through* the shape of the liturgy are boundless. The reflections that follow are not meant to be definitive, but are intended as sparks that may help get some sermon fires started.

ᘣ *Ash Wednesday: Dust without Dirt*

"I don't see why your church has a confession of sin every Sunday. Jesus died to take our sins away. Once we have asked God for forgiveness, we ought to take seriously the freedom from sin that God gives us. Sure, when we mess up, we will need to say 'I'm sorry' again. But having to confess your sins every time you come to church—that's a real drag!"

The sentiments of this young woman capture, I think, the conflicted feelings that many people have concerning the liturgy of Ash Wednesday: "I certainly don't claim to be perfect, but this is a little much! The put-downs and the dirt that others seem to throw in my direction are bad enough! Having to go up and get ashes smudged on my forehead—well, it just isn't very helpful."

Preoccupation with guilt or resistance to such preoccupation—one or both of these is quite likely to haunt potential participants in an Ash Wednesday service. What is a preacher to do with them? Or, rather, what is the preacher to do with the sermon in order to gain a hearing in the face of such pronounced psychological static? The preacher takes a cue, I think, from the following phrases that appear in the day's proper liturgy:

> ᘣ From the collect of the day: "Almighty and everlasting
> God, you hate nothing you have made."

∾ From Psalm 103, appointed for the service: "For [God] himself knows whereof we are made; he remembers that we are but dust."

∾ From the minister's invitation to the observance of a holy Lent: "All Christians continually have [the need] to renew their repentance and faith."

∾ From the prayer before the imposition of ashes: "that we may remember that it is only by your gracious gift that we are given everlasting life."

∾ From the rite of the imposition of ashes: "Remember that you are dust, and to dust you shall return."

The center of the Ash Wednesday service is repentance. Being called to repentance, however, does not mean being called on the carpet and put down. Repentance involves remembering:

∾ that God hates nothing that is made, and our own self-deprecations, as well as our put-downs of other people, are as unnecessary as they are wrong;

∾ what *God* remembers constantly with mercy and compassion: that we are but dust, fragile creatures whose failures consist in our misguided attempts at self-sufficiency rather than in our lack of success in achieving it;

∾ that God offers as gift the everlasting life that we strive to manufacture for ourselves.

In such a context, the confession of sin, the commitment to spiritual discipline, and the confession of our mortality in being marked with ashes are all expressions of the remembrance we undertake in response to *God's* gracious remembering of *us*. When we remember what God remembers—that we are dust—it becomes, for a time at least, less necessary for us to treat either ourselves or others like dirt.

It is the function of the Ash Wednesday sermon, therefore, to celebrate a divine grace that enables us to remember, amidst all our disastrous forgettings, the good that God made and will never hate. Psalm 51 and the Litany of Penitence, both of which follow the sermon and the imposition of ashes, can be a turning loose of the cramping death grip in which we hold our own egos. What freedom!

Some of these ideas were eloquently expressed in an Ash Wednesday sermon I heard not long ago. Here is an excerpt:

> Sin is not a popular word today. People complain that it smacks of judgmentalism and condemnation. But it is one of the most easily verified truths: people are sinful. No doubt there are conditions (many of which are the results of sin themselves) which make specific and harmful sins more likely. But the root cause of all of this is our human weakness—which should neither surprise nor depress us, but set us free.
>
> Ash Wednesday is a time where all pretense is stripped away. Where we are labeled as "dust." Where we become aware that we are utterly dependent on God for our very being. This frees us to be as good as we can be, while knowing that our salvation is not dependent on our actions, but on our relationship with Jesus Christ.
>
> "If we say we have no sin, we deceive ourselves, and the truth is not in us." It is when we start believing that we have control of our lives, and do not desire or feel we need God, that we place limits on what God can do for, in, and through us. Psalm 51 says that "the sacrifice of God is a troubled spirit." When our spirit is troubled by those things which are not of God, God can then come to us, face to face, desiring the best for us—and loving us as we are.

Notice how the preacher incorporates powerful lines from the scripture texts of the day—not explaining them, referring to them, or trying to improve upon them. Instead he uses the surrounding sermon language to provide a fresh approach to and through these texts, which otherwise might be heard as pure negativity.

In summary, Ash Wednesday does not warn: "If you start right now, and work very hard, maybe you can get the mess of your life cleaned up by Easter!" Rather, Ash Wednesday invites: "Take a deep breath, and a fresh look at the world God is relentlessly loving back into healthy dependence upon divine life! *Now,* what steps might we take, individually and as a community, to live in *that* direction? Thus in Ash Wednesday sermons we try to avoid and include the following principles.

Try to avoid:
- ∾ condemnations of "bad" or "sinful" behavior;
- ∾ abstract discussions of what to give up or take on for Lent;
- ∾ attempts to generate a guilt trip ("How can we be so rotten when God is so good?").

Try to include:
- ∾ engaging descriptions of a merciful and compassionate God who remembers;
- ∾ encouragement to let go of the ways in which we may be making a poor job of playing God.

∾ *Palm Sunday: Power without Control*
The Palm Sunday liturgy is beset by complexity and contradictions. Shouts of "Hosanna!" and "Crucify him!" are juxtaposed hard upon each other, a full passion narrative threatens to "steal the thunder" of the liturgy of Good Friday,

and a sensory overload of words and elaborate ceremony can numb the attention of the participants, many of whom have no intention of returning to church before Easter Sunday. What is a preacher to do in the face of such formidable factors? In a word, find a single, simple focus that can shape attention succinctly and in short order! This homiletical prescription applies to many other times and places, obviously, but it is particularly crucial here. Precisely *because* so much is going on, the impact of the service will be lost without a focal point that can only be provided through the sermon.

A frequently employed sermon strategy on this day is to do variations on a "the crowd was fickle and so are we" theme. There is, of course, much truth in that assertion. The difficulty is that such a strategy does not seem fully to accord with the thrust of the collects in the Liturgy of the Palms, which is less moralistic and more mysterious:

> Assist us mercifully with your help, O Lord God of our salvation, that we may enter with joy upon the contemplation of those mighty acts, whereby you have given us life and immortality.

> Let these branches be for us signs of his victory, and grant that we who bear them in his name may ever hail him as our King.

Contemplation of God's mighty acts may provide a more fruitful homiletical focus for this day, I think, than condemnation of misguided and culpable human ones. This is by no means to suggest that the high drama of denial and betrayal along the *via dolorosa* should be soft-peddled in the sermon for the day, nor the deeply ironic tension between "hosanna" and "crucify him" be avoided. But if God's mighty acts are the focus rather than human failings, those who come to church on Palm Sunday are more likely to be effectively brought into contact with "the mystery of our redemption." This mystery involves the striking fact that the Exalted One, who does not need either the cheers or the curses of the crowd, nevertheless makes himself vulnerable to both. Jesus is clearly misunderstood by those who organize the two parades into Jerusalem and up to Golgotha, and yet, ironically, both parades end up at points of significant truth about him. He *is* Sovereign Lord, even though not in the way that the strewers of palms envision. He *is* Suffering Servant, though he is not the sort of victim that everyone imagines they are crucifying. Jesus participates in both processions through the city—the one that seems to honor and the one that seems to degrade—but his identity is defined by neither.

The sermon can honor and enhance our experience and understanding of all that Palm Sunday places before us. While there is much more that can be offered in preaching to those who return for the services of Thursday, Friday, and Saturday, the message that comes through the liturgy of this day can effectively do its work even for those who will not come back to church until Easter morning.

These suggestions for highlighting "what makes this day different" are evident in the following Palm Sunday sermon from Luke's passion narrative, which readers from the congregation have just dramatically enacted. I shall briefly excerpt the sermon in "plot-line" form—that is, in the sequence of its dramatic conceptual movements.

> 1) What is compelling about the drama we have just reenacted? It is violent, but prime-time TV is packed with that. It is a moral outrage, but these are going on around us all the time. It is a saga of conflict and tragedy, but there's plenty of that at home and at the office. Why, then, does it have such distinctive and enduring power?

2) My eye is drawn to the One at the center of the storm. Jesus is the source of all the conflict, yet he is the only character who is composed and collected. All the rest—Judas, Peter, Caiaphas, Herod—are "beside themselves."

3) These other characters are all in conflict with Jesus because they are in conflict with themselves. When they confront Jesus, they also come face to face with who they are. Jesus forces each into a moment of truth.

4) What is a "moment of truth"? Not simply a discovery of important new information. Rather, a situation in which circumstances back you into a corner. You discover that you have been playing the game both ways, serving two masters, both having and eating your cake. Suddenly you have to make a choice—one which both reveals and creates the person you really are.

5) In each case, Jesus forces the option, not by manipulating their behavior, but by standing before them in such a way that their response can no longer be ambiguous.

6) But there is another possible meaning of "moment of truth"—a situation in which, under fire, the best of who you are can shine forth in utter clarity and for great good. And this is the moment of truth into which Jesus gives his life: "Father, forgive them."

7) Jesus' moment of truth makes possible a similar moment for the centurion and for us. Today we say neither the confession of sin, nor the confession of faith. That is not because it would make the service too long.

Rather, in playing the crowd in the passion narrative, we have confessed our sin, and in accepting Jesus' radical forgiveness, we do confess our faith. Faced with a "moment of truth" (sense one), today can be for us, through Jesus Christ, a "moment of truth" (sense two).

In its measured, reflective way, the flow of this sermon attempts to complement the distinctive liturgical elements of the day, rather than competing with or capitulating to them. The sermon also tries indirectly to acknowledge the cries of both "Hosanna" and "Crucify him," which have been prominent earlier in the liturgy. The preacher is trying here to embody homiletical principles appropriate to this day that may be summarized as follows.

Try to avoid:
- ∾ abstract moralizing, extended theologizing, or pious generalizing about the passion of Jesus or the depravity of those (then or now) who crucify him.

Try to include:
- ∾ sharp, succinct descriptions (perhaps through particular scenes, characters, images, or actions) of how, in the passion of Jesus, God is redemptively present to all the conflicting forces that vie for control of human affairs;
- ∾ an inviting sense of how the mystery of our redemption will be further perceived and celebrated in the liturgies of the coming week.

∾ Maundy Thursday: Servanthood without Servitude

The resistance of many persons and parishes to the liturgy of footwashing is proverbial. Perhaps it is simply that people feel that their feet are too ugly or ticklish, but I suspect it goes much deeper than that. Shaking hands with someone is an accepted social practice, one that can be done quite impersonally. While a handshake often signals cordiality, even welcome, it seldom leads to a significant level of openness, let alone intimacy. With feet, however, it is an altogether different matter. Touching another's feet, or placing one's feet in the hands of another, is not (like shaking hands) an expression of equality; it is an expression of vulnerability. A certain submission to the other is entailed, whether you offer your own feet or receive the feet of someone else into your hands. A certain inequality is even more evident in such interchanges than it is in an embrace.

It is not coincidental, I think, that the liturgy on this day unites two themes, one found in the synoptic gospels (as well as in 1 Corinthians), and the other found in the gospel of John. These are Jesus' institution of the eucharist and his washing of the disciples' feet. Both are acts of great communal intimacy, and both evoke an almost visceral reaction: "Wash my *feet?!* Eat your *flesh* and drink your *blood?!* You can't be serious!" Putting these two together is almost more than our minds (or stomachs) can take. The thrust of the liturgy, however, is to assault the well-defended walls of both in a strategic attempt to reach us at our hearts. This purpose will be sidetracked if the sermon of the day is a lecture about either of the liturgical actions, one that holds forth on "the meaning of the eucharist" or "the importance of radical servanthood." What we need to be about as preachers in this service is a further deepening of what was begun on Palm Sunday, a sense of the mystery of our redemption.

What does it mean to participate with Jesus in a form of service, which, whether given or received, has absolutely nothing servile about it? All too often the bottom line of the message on this day is simplistic: "Jesus served you, so get on out there and serve others!" Such preaching does not foster the sense of a healthy humility that Jesus had, one that honors all who participate.

Far and away the most powerful Maundy Thursday sermon I have ever experienced was delivered by a woman with a keen sense of the multidimensional dynamics at work in her congregation on this day. She began by inviting everyone to remove their shoes, if they wished. After all, their feet were "hot, tired, and pinched from a long day in uncomfortable shoes." Didn't God tell Moses to take off his shoes on holy ground? "Well, this too is holy ground."

With a twinkle in her eye, the preacher then speculated that Adam and Eve must have gone shoeless in the garden of Eden—touching with their bare toes the humus from which humans were created. Rocks, thistles, tree roots, broken glass, rusty nails, as well as bunions, corns, hammertoes, fungus infections, and fallen arches all came after the Fall—and with them came the feeling that feet are embarrassing.

The preacher then shifted the scene to Jesus' day, where hospitality from a host involved removing the sandals and bathing the hot, dusty feet of his guests—a humble task, usually delegated to servants or wives. This humble service has already been offered to Jesus, said the preacher, by Mary of Bethany, who has not only washed his feet, but also anointed them and wiped them with her hair. "Jesus, too, has been honored in this humble way." Now Jesus does the same for his disciples, first pausing (as John's gospel says) to remember who he is—coming from God and going to God. "The act of service grows out of knowing who he is, and where he is going."

Peter protests the footwashing, and the preacher could identify with this, having been taught since childhood that "it is more blessed to give than to receive." Yet the message of humility Jesus is teaching has as much to do with receiving as with giving. As Jesus tells Peter: "Unless I wash you, you have no share with me—you can't give what you haven't got." "If we don't know humility," the preacher said, "we risk bringing humiliation."

A story followed. A "terribly proper" woman who ventures out on a San Francisco street too soon after a bout with pneumonia collapses on the sidewalk, utterly helpless. People walk by, ignoring her. Finally, a "very dirty and rather aromatic little old man" comes up and asks if she needs help. The woman clutches her purse and nods. He leaves, returns with a street colleague, and both of them assist her to her car. The woman later speaks of how hard it was for her to accept help from these two fellow creatures.

Then the preacher brought the sermon home:

> When or where do we ever find ourselves on the ground? Can we recognize the ground when we're sitting on it? Can we humbly accept the gift of an outstretched hand, or two hands washing our feet? Or the gift of life, offered for us?

Jesus knew who he was, he was grounded in his identity. He knew his origins and where he was going. And he invites us to join him on that journey. If we're going to "go and do likewise," we too have to know who we are, where we've come from, and where we're going.

Think back to Ash Wednesday, when we began this journey with a cross marked on our foreheads. We heard the words "Remember that you are dust, and to dust you shall return." Lent is a journey that begins in dusty ashes. We're dust—made from the earth. We are created beings, earthlings, dependent upon the one who creates us. If we lose our sense of groundedness in God—that humility—we have nothing to share with others. We have no common ground. We have to have our feet firmly planted before we can love and serve others.

Come have your feet washed, as we prepare to walk

the way of the cross. Come feel your earthy, humble roots, and be strengthened for the journey. Feet don't need to be embarrassing. They're the part of us that's closest to the ground. They're the most human, and perhaps the most to be honored. Come let your feet, and yourself, be honored. Come receive this gift of love. Humbly offered, let it be humbly received.

The end of the sermon led directly into the liturgy of footwashing; by then, it was almost impossible not to join in. The sermon did not coerce, but rather invited us into full and free participation. Participation that, in all probability, was not restricted to the time and place of the rite conducted in the sanctuary. This sermon did much more than teach us *about* the relation between words "humus" and "humility." It did not dodge touchy issues, utter platitudes, or issue moralistic injunctions. It led us *through* the scripture, *through* the liturgy, and *through* our scruples about intimacy and social distance. I would love to be able to preach like that on Maundy Thursday!

Insofar as we can work toward such an ideal, we can:

Try to avoid:

ை abstractions about the importance of humility and service;

ை reflections on the eucharist that come across like written food recipes, instead of engaging the listeners and drawing them to participate, like appetizers before a rich banquet.

Try to include:

ை a reverence for and identification with the One who calls us friends;

༜ a sense of what Jesus means by friendship in the two striking and complementary "hands-on" actions of footwashing and feeding.

༜ *Good Friday: Suffering without Sentimentality*

"Christians," said Teilhard de Chardin, "are not called to swoon in the shadow of the cross, but to climb in its light." Good Friday services, however, sometimes seem to facilitate the former more than the latter. An extended liturgy is surely appropriate. One gets the feeling, however, that the underlying purpose of those who gather is vague at best: "If Jesus suffered for three hours, the least we can do is hang around the church for as long as he hung there on the cross!"

It is not unusual for services held on this day to be emotionally somber, even intense. And surely there is nothing wrong with that: we are, after all, dealing here with matters of cosmic gravity. But swooning in the face of these matters will not do any good:

༜ "Poor, poor Jesus!"

༜ "Rotten, no good me!"

༜ "Oh, how both of us have suffered!"

༜ "All the anguish of the world—it's enough to break your heart!"

༜ "Damn the evil everywhere!"

These and similar sentiments will surely lurk in the corners of everyone's mind on Good Friday. Such feelings will need to be acknowledged, at least in the preacher's preparation, but they do not have to be nourished in the preaching event.

This is not at all to say that the Good Friday service is no place for the healthy expression of grief and suffering. It is not unusual at funeral services for those attending to find themselves grieving "in two time zones at once," as a friend of mine once aptly put it. Grief (like other emotions) is not a "thing" but a process. Particularly when the setting clearly invites it, we may well feel the pain of other losses in addition to, or even instead of the one for which the requiem of the day is the immediate occasion. An analogous dynamic can operate on Good Friday. The question is: how can the sermon on this day enable those who hear it to climb in the light of the cross rather than to swoon in its shadow?

Again, a cue is given by the shape and flow of the liturgy:

- ∾ The Passion Gospel from St. John
- ∾ The Sermon
- ∾ The Solemn Collects
- ∾ The Veneration of the Cross
- ∾ The Reception of Communion from the Reserved Sacrament.

In John's passion story, Jesus is clearly in possession of himself and in charge of the situation. The other players in the drama—Pilate, the chief priests, the disciples, the crowd—are at the mercy of their own fears, angers, and ambitions. Jesus alone is not a victim in the situation. His is an utterly *active* passion. "No one takes my life from me," he has said earlier. "I give it of my own free will. I have power to lay it down, and I have power to take it up again." If Jesus does not swoon in the shadow of his own cross, perhaps our sermons should not, either. The penitential season, begun on Ash Wednesday, is the place for self-examination, contrition, and honest confession. "Aren't you sorry for what you've done to me" is *not* one of the "last words" of Jesus from the cross!

Particularly if we pay attention to the language of the Solemn Collects and the Veneration of the Cross, both unique to the Good Friday liturgy, it is evident that the focus of this service is something very different: grateful adoration for the saving work of Jesus and commitment to participate with him in the specific sufferings which, as the author of Colossians suggests (1:24), are a necessary and still unfinished part of the mystery of our redemption.

The Solemn Collects identify, in turn, the people for whom we pray "according to their needs":

- ∾ "the holy Catholic Church of Christ throughout the world";
- ∾ "all nations and peoples of the earth, and for those in authority among them";
- ∾ "all who suffer and are afflicted in body or in mind";
- ∾ "all who have not received the Gospel of Christ";
- ∾ ourselves, in communion with "all who have departed this world and have died in the peace of Christ."

The final Solemn Collect powerfully identifies the love that hangs on the cross with the love that is constantly remaking the world. On Good Friday, in other words, we celebrate "what wondrous love is this!" and, through prayer and adoration, we initiate a liturgy inside the church that cannot be contained within its walls. In sharing the Reserved Sacrament, we "become one with the One we receive."

The following sermon for Good Friday attempts to incorporate these ideas through the unifying concept of *perspective.* Again, I have given excerpts of the sermon in plot-line form:

1) Whenever someone is caught up in the thick of things, they may have difficulty seeing the "big picture." What they need, we say, is "perspective." Friends or counselors may offer such perspective, but often that assistance is unhelpful because it is perceived as being too general or abstract. The one who purports to "have perspective" is not "in touch" with the real life circumstances.

2) It can be a different matter when the advice-giver is caught in a similar bind. Somehow, now, the

abstractions don't seem to fit. The credibility of the "perspective" previously offered is thereby rendered suspect.

3) In John's gospel, Jesus is forever putting things in perspective for those who are too close to their respective situations—for example, Nicodemus, the Woman at the Well, the Blind Man and his temple antagonists, Mary and Martha at the tomb of Lazarus (all treated in the Sunday gospel lessons during the season of Lent). What, then, is it like for Jesus when he himself is in the thick of things?

4) It is striking that in this, the most "philosophical" gospel, Jesus explicitly expresses his own needs ("I thirst") and his care for those close to him ("Woman, behold your son"). This Jesus is the eternal Word made human flesh. His perspective is credible precisely because he knows what it feels like to be human. (A brief correlation is made with the epistle lesson from Hebrews 10.)

5) A story is told of the preacher's earnest but ineffectual attempts to comfort a man whose fiancée had just been tragically killed. Comfort came to the man only when he encountered another person who had suffered a similar loss. Likewise, in the cross Jesus, our high priest and Incarnate Word, comes to comfort us.

6) Once you have been comforted like that, it is the most natural thing in the world to offer comfort as you have been comforted. The Solemn Collects can serve as the first move we make to share with others in the sufferings,

the perspective, and the comfort of Christ which is bound up in the cross.

In sermons on Good Friday, therefore, we:

Try to avoid:

- ∾ outdoing the drama of the passion gospel by attempting to retell it after it has just been read in its entirety;
- ∾ abstract moralizing or theologizing (just as on Palm Sunday) about suffering or the cross;
- ∾ sentimentality that encourages listeners to indulge in "swooning" over the cross.

Try to include:

- ∾ a celebration of the powerful grace of a vulnerable God, which is perfected in suffering for and with the whole human family;
- ∾ a vision of "things that were cast down are being raised up," and "things that had grown old are being made new" through the creative, suffering love of God in Jesus Christ.

∾ *Easter Vigil: Tradition without Imprisonment*

"Who are you?" We are closer to a deeper truth about ourselves when we answer that question by sharing some of our personal stories and our family history than we are when we fill in a form to get a driver's license or a credit card. We are better revealed to ourselves and to others by the story lines through which our experience has unfolded, and by the spaces that those story lines provide for conversation and reflection.

The Easter Vigil is the time and the place in which the Christian community, through chapter after chapter of scripture, reveals and celebrates its identity in the language of sacred story. How sad for a congregation if they are denied the opportunity of this service, or if they are simply subjected to what either feels like a boring set of interminable readings or the Reader's Digest "condensed version." The readings of this service are not so many liturgical hoops to jump en route to the first eucharist of Easter; the psalms are not just an occasion for music history buffs to relish in the glories of plainsong or Anglican chant. This is a liturgical place where time stands still, so that we can hear, see, taste, touch, and smell the sense of holiness that surrounds us in the recounting of our sacred history.

Baptism, the renewal of baptismal vows, and the "Alleluia" proclaiming that "Christ is Risen!" take place at other times than the Easter Vigil. In this service, however, these significant liturgical acts find their full grounding. This is (or can be) a celebration of tradition at its quintessential best—not the dead hand of enslaving tradition, but a possibility for tangible reconnection with that mighty hand of God which is always reaching out to break oppression, set captives free, and signal in redemptive action the Jubilee of God's gracious favor.

It is important, as the preacher at this service, not to compete with the mystery of darkness and candlelight, the music of psalms and anthems, or the exuberance of resurrection joy. The task of the sermon is to give shape to all of these. In such a lengthy service, it is also important (to state the obvious) that the sermon be short, and that it *be* a celebration, rather than a discussion of whether, why, and how to celebrate. Imagine a party that consisted merely of *talking* about the importance of parties, and the special importance of this one!

We celebrate God's "freedom moves" homiletically by making *analogous* sermon moves—not by repeating the stories that have just been read, but by finding a way that resonates with their theme and thrust. Sermon listeners need to experience the potent stranglehold of enslaving forces that, while already conquered by resurrection power, are still vigorously at work. They also need to experience how the risen Christ is even now setting people free in ways that catch them off guard and raise them to new life, just as the first day of resurrection stunned and galvanized the defeated and disoriented disciples.

One good story leads to another—that is a part of the mystery of our redemption. That sense of mystery can be facilitated in the sermon at an Easter Vigil.

Let me share with you an Easter Vigil preaching situation I found myself in a few years ago. The parish was a well-to-do but rather sparse city congregation insulated from the dynamics of poverty and crime that surrounded them; in fact, just a few days before, in the middle of Holy Week, there had been a fatal shooting at a nearby mall. The rector was trying to establish the Easter Vigil service as a norm in the parish worship life. An infant baptism was scheduled; the last time the parents had come to church was the baptism of the infant's older brother. Biblical literacy among the members of the congregation was not high, and I was profoundly struck by how far removed the Vigil passages would sound to their ears, but also how closely the themes of despair and need to which these scriptures initially spoke resonated both with unspoken issues in the parish and with concerns in my own life. The challenge was clear—how could this Vigil sermon do in its context what the scriptures did in theirs?

The following sermon is what unfolded, as I tried to listen for what made this day different.

> "Come and see!...Go and tell!"
> An earthquake erupts, an angel descends and deposits itself on a giant boulder. Shaking a few traces of dust

from snow white clothing, the angel fixes you firmly with a piercing gaze, then utters the Easter invitation: "Come and see! Then go and tell!" What do you say to a mighty angel who is staring you straight in the eye?

Is all this "angel" language making you a bit uncomfortable? Okay, try the exercise another way.

Daybreak on Easter morning. The sun blazes up from the horizon, banishing the darkness, bathing the world in brilliance. What do we see? What shall we say?

I'll speak for myself. Here's my first, spontaneous reaction: "Will somebody please cut the lights? I'd rather not see things quite so clearly, thank you just the same. Everywhere I look, from Johannesburg to Mogadishu, from cities under seize in Bosnia to Thursday's senseless shooting spree in the O Street market—everywhere I look there is desolate valley, and it is full of bones....And they are very dry. *That's* what I see—and that's about all I can say. Even on Easter morning."

My eyes are sorely in need of fresh vision—are yours? And that is why you and I have come together on this holy night, is it not? Because we need to see the world with fresh eyes. Not to deny the anguish all around us; but to see it in the light of Jesus' resurrection.

Our senses have been washed over this evening with the sights and sounds of sacred myth. Maybe that makes us nervous, even as it touches a longing deep within. But we do not have a choice tonight between language that is myth-shaped and language that is myth-free. Our only options are between myths of creation and myths of devastation, myths of hope and myths of despair.

Facts—that's what we want. But what counts as "facts," you see, depends a lot on whether your point of reference is an empty tomb, or a valley of dry bones.

"Our bones are dried up, and our hope is lost; we are cut off completely!" Those are the facts for the children of Israel, as they despair under Babylonian captivity in the age of the prophet Ezekiel. And those are the facts now—bitterly wept over, or quietly choked on—by children young and old the world over, by those who are captive to violence, poverty, uneasy affluence, and increasingly abortive attempts at social planning: "Our bones are dried up, and our hope is lost; we are cut off completely." Do you hear it? It is the language of despairing imagination. A vision of reality that holds it hostage in a desperate death-grip.

Suddenly, a question cracks across the valley, not from the bones, or from the prophet, but from the Almighty One: "Mortal! Can these bones live?" "Oh Lord God, you know!" Ezekiel gasps—hardly daring to hope—having nary a clue as to what there is to hope for. But God, it seems, has a more fertile imagination. And, if what we have rehearsed tonight in sacred song and story is any indication, a fertile imagination is a fairly reliable trademark of God's distinctive style.

"Let there be!" says God. And it is so. A world comes into being—shimmering and pulsing with life. And when God sees what God has made—fish and fowl, flora and fauna, woman and man—behold, it is very good.

"Can these bones live?" A God who can raise *that* question is a God who can raise up an answer beyond the wildest of human imaginings. The word and breath that bring life out of chaos can speak and act in the valley of dry bones to rob desert graves of their prey.

But this time, in the valley of dry bones, there is a different twist. In creation, God did it all alone. Now God invites Ezekiel to share in the sacred act of energizing. "Prophesy to these bones, Ezekiel! Tell them to listen up. Tell them they are going to get reconnected. Tell them that, not by human might, or by clever human planning, but by my Spirit, they will live."

God speaks, and it is so, and it is good. Myth becomes fact. Dry bones stand upon the earth and live at the word of the Lord through the word of the prophet. Broken and battered and bereft of hope, Israel does indeed return home from its captivity—just as God said. Who would ever have imagined!

"Come and see! Then go and tell!" the angel urges. "The risen one is going before you. Go on! Try to catch up with him!—Too late! He's caught up with you instead!

"Greetings! Do not be afraid! Go and tell the good news to my sisters and brothers—yes, that's who you are, for all of you are forgiven and freed. It is so! Let it be! It is good!"

Into this wild resurrection dance tonight comes Oliver George. Simply to be given a rite of social initiation? Hardly! Merely to be certified as a religious statistic? I should say not! Oliver is being welcomed right into the heart of God's loving imagination. God imagines Oliver as God's own special possession—and it is so.

"Say the words, pour the water," God commands us the community of St. John's Church. "Pour the water, sign his forehead; I will make him Christ's own forever. And behold, it is *very* good!"

In Jesus Christ, God enters death itself—staggering under its weight, suffering under its blows, sharing in its grief. Doing death—and undoing it—once and for all uniting us in his death and pledging to us a share in his resurrection.

It is so. And it is good. The message is, in fact, for us: Alleluia! Christ is risen! Come and see! Go and tell!

This Easter Vigil sermon, of course, has a very different feel to it than the one in chapter five. That simply attests to the fact that working under the disciplining constraints of special occasions by no means restricts the preacher's creativity. What will *not* work is a sermonic analysis of, or reflection upon, the liturgical rites and rubrics that are "proper" to the day. In sermons at the Easter Vigil, therefore:

Try to avoid:

ॐ talking about the scriptural stories or giving simple summaries of them, to say nothing of drawing morals from them.

Try to include:

ॐ a judicious selection and weaving of images, actions, or motifs from the scripture stories appointed for the liturgy that can offer an experience of resurrection power touching and transforming the tombs and prisons of human experience.

CHAPTER EIGHT

Christmas and Easter, Epiphany and Pentecost

Preaching Grace through Festival Celebrations

Preaching on Christmas Eve and Easter Day is, as Charles Dickens wrote in *A Tale of Two Cities*, "the best of times and the worst of times." It is the best of times. Festival celebrations of the incarnation of Jesus and of his resurrection are the primal sources of all that the church is about. Attendance is seldom, if ever, higher than on these two special days. Music, flowers, banners, and candlelight—all the stops are pulled out. A sense of energy and expectation is palpable. Who would not want to preach at a time like this?

They are the worst of times because, for openers, the high attendance at these services is a decidedly mixed blessing. Why do people show up in such numbers? Motivations are many, complex, and conflicting: uncritical accommodation to social custom, grudging participation in family ritual as a means of maintaining domestic peace, vaguely felt guilt for not having come to church more frequently, inarticulate spiritual hunger, expectation of a spiritual "peak" experience, memories of previous holidays. And, sometimes, a deep desire for a fitting culmination to an Advent/Lenten

103

journey, together with a determination to carry the celebration forward into the ensuing season—the Twelve Days of Christmas, or the Great Fifty Days of Easter. Regardless of their convictions or predispositions, however, many people come to church on these days carrying heavy agendas of anguish: major holidays have a way of triggering instant access to major pain.

Those who seldom come to church may well expect to be either catered to or censored on these two days. Those who attend regularly will hope both for a sense of continuity and reassurance with respect to their spiritual journeys, and for fresh insight, inspiration, and challenge. To shape a sermon with the potential of touching people in all (or even in some) of these places is definitely a tall order. How can sermons on these days help listeners to (in Marcus Borg's fine phrase) "meet Jesus again for the first time"? Is there any point of contact among the many kinds of people who come to these special services?

Perhaps there is. While most of us have at best inadequate understandings of birth, death, and resurrection life, we do have, as theologian Terry Holmes used to say, a "deep memory" that can be stirred by the nativity and resurrection stories. On these two days it is not so much the liturgies laid down in prayer books and church worship manuals that provide the focus through which the sermon most effectively moves; rather, it is the liturgies implicitly written in the pages of human experience that can best facilitate the sermon.

That claim may spark an objection: what about the distinctive witness to Jesus Christ presented in the scriptures? Apart from the story materials offered there (and the theological reflection in scripture and Christian tradition that attends them), there is little upon which to base a celebration. "Newborn babies are endearing," and "Flowers return in the spring" may be true enough, but if that is all "Merry

Christmas!" and "Happy Easter!" mean in the "deep memory" of participants, then the extra effort that goes into these two worship services is wasted energy.

Yes, the witness of scripture is of critical importance on these days. The answers scripture offers to our deepest human longings need to be set forth clearly, not simply given a homiletical "spin" or a festive flavoring that caters, smorgasbord style, to the various appetites of those present. And yet the "good for you" alternative seldom generates much interest in eating. The question is: how can essential nourishment be offered in ways that engage the appetite?

Perhaps the preacher can take a cue from a theme that recurs in all of the gospel accounts concerning both the birth and the resurrection of Jesus: the appearance of the *unexpected* in the most *unlikely* of circumstances. The continual retelling of these stories, itself essential for Christian identity, cannot help but result in a sanding down and smoothing out of their astonishing "rough edges." The incarnation of God comes in the form of an illegitimate child; the birth announcements come to lowlife shepherds and pagan foreigners. The risen Christ appears to women, whose testimony was of no legal value, and is subsequently proclaimed by "ignorant, unlearned men." Our astonishment at such doings, after countless retellings over many generations, is (understandably) a bit thin. A story whose ending we know already is no longer astonishing. The wonder of it all is a bit cozy. The primal experience, however, was anything but cozy for all of the parties involved. Instead, it turned their world upside down. How can the Christmas or Easter sermon not simply repeat the information given in scripture, but recreate the impact of those earth-shattering events?

The objective in a sermon for Christmas Eve or Easter Day is not to shock listeners or jerk them around; neither will these sermons simply say (with glowing feeling): "We all know what's coming down here—and ain't it just grand!" Rather, the sermon will try to take people, regardless of where they happen to be, from "Yes, I know what this is about" to "My God, I never imagined!" New Testament scholar and preacher Fred Craddock describes this dynamic as a movement from "the nod of recognition" to "the shock of recognition."

How can the preacher on Christmas or Easter do that? By imaginatively listening for how grace might similarly become incarnate in the lives of gathered listeners who know, but don't know. By envisioning the dramatic possibilities and the thrust of new life bursting through the graveyard of intractable hopelessness in the here and now. This cannot be done apart from an understanding of the relevant texts in scripture, but that understanding will have to be in intimate conversation with the strains and struggles of people's lives, in the midst of which the incarnate, risen Lord is also present, but not recognized. The stories of Christmas and Easter, in other words, cannot be summarized and "applied." Those in the congregation will have to be *shown* Christmas and Easter, not just "talked to" about them.

Listen in on parts of one preacher's attempt to do just that.

It was getting late on Christmas Eve and I was caught in heavy traffic on my way to do the last of my Christmas shopping. There was snow in the air, and brightly colored decorations beamed down from light poles. I rushed from my car, knowing that I had precious little time to get everything I needed. As I walked up to the busy department store, I noticed the small figure sitting huddled against the side of the building. Drawing closer, I saw the dirty sign around the person's neck. The message was very simple, just two words: Merry Christmas! There were no appeals for charity; there was only a simple proclamation from someone who lived on the streets in poverty, amid the filth and dangers of a big city. A message made from crayon on a piece of cardboard from someone who had little to be merry about. It filled me with wonder.

Crayon on dirty cardboard. Simple words proclaiming "Merry Christmas." A very ordinary person announcing the presence of Christ in the world. Christ's presence from the beginning and to this very day is directed to the places of pain and hurt, brokenness and hunger.

God did not choose to come to earth at the highest point of life, but at its lowest point. God did not choose to enter the safe world of decorated churches and hallowed sanctuaries; instead, God chose to enter the rough-and-tumble world of people with jobs to do, fields to tend, and government breathing down their backs at tax time.

God is not above and beyond our need and reach. Tonight God is revealed to us in a manger stall, and also by a message printed on a dirty piece of cardboard. In Christ, God loves us and is with us wherever we are. Christ is born: let us glorify him. Let us go out to meet him.

A tangible way of "showing" Christmas and Easter to a congregation is through the music, colorful vestments, and pageants that accompany these feasts. Music and sanctuary adornment are not simply "special effects" for the theological drama of these special days. Although stimulating to the senses and the emotions, these worship elements are debased if their role is merely to release a flow of sentimental religious energy. Along with the sermon, music and festival appointments are sacred art forms in which the meaning of incarnation and resurrection can be richly embodied. It goes without saying that all of these art forms must be orchestrated through the careful efforts of all the ministers involved.

It is easy either to accommodate or to condemn all the accretions to these holy days that have become cultural holidays as well. This subject takes us in the direction of issues we will address in the next two chapters. At this juncture it is appropriate to say, however, that much of the finger-shaking at the "commercialization" of Christmas and Easter that denies their "true meaning" is highly selective. The supposedly counter-cultural theology served up in "we are (or should be) holier than they are" sermons can itself be as sentimental and culture-cozy as a Hallmark card. How nice that the birth announcement came to "lowly shepherds." But how welcoming, in fact, is the church today to those in society who are also on society's outer margins? How willing has the church been to honor the ministerial authority of women, who were the first proclaimers of the gospel?

Of course the hype and hoopla that surround both Easter and Christmas can be distracting and profoundly dangerous. And yet, while there are all manner of counterfeit elements in these celebrations, the celebrations themselves can, and often do, suggest *both* a longing for grace and its manifestation as well. Before preachers engage in indiscriminate railing, they perhaps should consider whether what they are railing against might be itself, in fact, an expression of very unexpected grace that it is their calling to point out and proclaim. Even the longing to exchange gifts and to celebrate new life with new clothes can have profound theological significance—and potential for redemption as well.

To summarize, in Christmas and Easter sermons:

Try to avoid:

ᗄ abstractions about the "meaning" of the events;

> ∾ harangues about what is or isn't "Christian" in a celebration of Christmas or Easter;
>
> ∾ a religious romanticism that will only add to the burdens many people carry as they come to church.

Try to include:

> ∾ a fresh, vigorous expression of the unlikely grace that may bring unexpected encounters with the incarnate, risen Lord.

∾ *Epiphany and Pentecost*

The feasts of Epiphany and Pentecost are not as highly charged as those of Christmas and Easter because they are free of the commercialism and of many of the painful emotions that may go along with the other two events. They have something else in common, too: each marks the culmination of the season begun by what many describe as the "bigger" feast. Epiphany concludes the Twelve Days of Christmas and Pentecost the Great Fifty Days of Easter. Both of these feasts expand the unfolding impact of the major feast preceding them. Epiphany celebrates the manifestation of Jesus as the Christ to those who live outside the boundaries of his own territory, and Pentecost, of course, does the same, as the descending tongues of fire enable Parthians, Medes, Elamites, residents of Mesopotamia, and many others to hear about God's deeds of power in their own language. So what might all of this mean for preaching on these two feast days?

One suggestion comes to mind: on either of these days, both of which so clearly celebrate the communal, conversational, cosmopolitan character of the gospel, it would be very odd for the sermon to be a religious monologue. This does not necessarily mean that on these occasions we will dispense with preaching as usual in favor of a meandering "dialogue sermon." Yet what better time for a preacher, in the spirit of the special day, not to talk *about* the communal nature of gospel proclamation or to issue a series of directives about witnessing for Jesus, but to talk *through* the lens of Epiphany and Pentecost to those who have come to hear the Good News?

What might that mean? How might it take shape? Perhaps by putting listeners in touch with some of the exciting ways that proclaiming the gospel is the vocation of all those baptized into Christ's body. How stimulating it might be to hear of ways in which, through word and action, the love of God is being translated in practical ways into the experience of those who otherwise would dismiss the whole religious enterprise as nothing more than pious, unintelligible talk. How reassuring it can be for a congregation to learn that forms of expression that are strange, even alien to their own ears, might well be complementary expressions of the gospel coming from those who have different gifts and functions in the one body. What a relief, if our success in gospel proclamation does not have to be measured by whether those who received it talk, think, act, and look just like us! Perhaps in our sermons about "wise men," "tongues of fire," and "many members/different gifts/one body" we preachers sometimes do not take these themes with as deep a homiletical seriousness as we could.

To preach with such a vision would be to do far more than simply honor events in an ancient biblical narrative; it would be to play the narrative "live" in a way that brings spectators onto the stage, and into the center of the action. In the sermon excerpted below you will sense a dialogue—not only between "us here and now" and "them back then," but between where we are now and where we long to be, and perhaps even between our voices and the voice of the Spirit.

Your first reaction to Pentecost may well be that
    there's little place for you in that upper room.
But above the jostle and hum of the seekers
    we sit in our quiet space.
We're the local people, ordinary people.
No super spirits.
Over there, Simon Peter, business entrepreneur,
    with his small fleet of fishing boats.
Next to him, Matthew, bureaucrat and tax man,
    on leave from his regional office near Jericho.
Then there's Simon the Zealot, political activist,
    good organizer and motivator.
And on around the room: James, John, Andrew,
    and the other disciples, and the women,
    and about a hundred others.
Capable, sensible people.
People you might see any morning at the 7:37 train,
    in business suits with attaché cases, bound for the
    Loop.
Ordinary people waiting for Pentecost
    up there above the seeking millions.

So we sit and wait.
We sit with Christ's promise,
    not sure what that
    Spirit will look or feel like
    when Pentecost happens.
All we know is that Christ promised
    to empower us for mission
    and so we wait prayerfully, expectantly, silently.

Then, the Spirit breaks loose.
God's order explodes into our order.
A deafening, thundering sound like a Kansas tornado.

A rush of warm wind slams us all into a huddle,
    making our hair stand on end.
Crackling streaks of flame pop and dance
    about our heads as we clutch at one another
    in fear and awe.
Finally, the swirl of heat and thunder above our heads
    turns into a pressure cooker within us that explodes
    in acts we never knew we were capable of.
Now we're on our feet, tumbling down the stairs,
    driven by the Spirit out into the melee of seekers
    in the streets below.
Surprising words start tumbling from our mouths.
We're talking other people's language,
    standing there eye-to-eye with Parthians, Medes,
    Pamphylians, Romans, Cretans, Arabians,
    telling them about the wholeness God gives,
    putting it in their own thought frame,
    their own symbol system, their own language.
The Spirit has driven you and me
    out of our prayer room
    to help seekers find wholeness.
That's Pentecost!

Now look again today out the windows
    of that upper room.
The Parthians, the Medes, the Pamphylians
    are still down there in our streets,
    hungering for wholeness,
    pilgrims in search of inner peace.
Up here in this room you and I wait again for the Spirit,
    not really feeling special, spiritually.
We're capable people. But ordinary people—
    in the things of the Spirit.
The wholeness isn't there.

We don't really have our act together.
Our spouses could tell you that.
Some people at the office could tell you that.
Surely we're capable enough to have enjoyed
    some power in our friendships.
But we know there's a wholeness that's missing.
Where's the Pentecost that will open the flow
    of personal, emotional, and spiritual power within us?

And then the Spirit breaks loose.
God's order explodes into our order
    like a tornado rearranging the landscape
        of our psyche,
    like cleansing fire spreading through our souls.

Now, in similar language, the preacher suggests a number
of different ways in which what feels like total destruction
might well be used by God as the cleansing power of the Holy
Spirit: the disintegration or painful rearrangement of a
marriage, the discovery that a son or daughter is gay or
lesbian, the loss of a career.

However your Pentecost begins,
    the pattern is so often the same.
Wind and fire shake your whole space,
    and traumatize you and me into new perceptions.
We're beginning to see what it looks like
    to be human beings,
        to respond to God's Spirit in our lives.
We're beginning to see the Spirit
    move us toward wholeness.

Then comes the climax of this contemporary Pentecost.
The swirl of wind and fire above our heads
    turns into a pressure cooker within us

that explodes into action
    we never knew we were capable of.
At some point we're on our feet, down the stairs,
    reaching out to seekers in the streets below.
And what's amazing is how readily and naturally
    you can speak the language of those seekers,
    to share with another seeker
      in his or her own language
      the gift of wholeness.
What a gift of the Holy Spirit to be able to do that!
Look how speaking in other tongues happens today.
To speak another's language is to enter deeply
    into that other person's world to promote wholeness.

Now, once again, the preacher elaborates some possibilities. Maybe you are a surgeon who becomes interested in healing the whole person rather than simply removing disease. Maybe you are the first woman executive in a corporation, led to reshape the company's policies so that everyone has a sense of ownership. Or a lawyer working for high-paying clients who feels called instead to defend those who haven't got a dime. Then the sermon concludes:

So, seeker, do you wonder if there's a place
    for you in the upper room?
Well, think again—
Feel the wind of the Spirit against your face.
Feel the fire of the Spirit spread through your soul.
And listen, seeker, to how you're beginning to speak.
You're offering the gift of wholeness.
Pentecost has come!
And it comes again and again.[1]

Notice, here, some principles at work that can make for effective preaching on Epiphany and Pentecost:

Try to avoid:

∾ telling a story or providing an analysis about an event disconnected from the community that has gathered to celebrate the feast.

Try to include:

∾ evoking an experience of the outpouring of the Spirit in speech that is as varied and creative as the gifted imaginations of the listeners, who are equally ministers of the Word;

∾ an emphasis on the communal aspects of proclaiming the gospel.

Endnote

1. The full sermon from which these portions are excerpted appears in "Preaching as the Interface of Two Social Worlds: The Congregation as Corporate Agent in the Act of Preaching" by Don Wardlaw, in *Preaching as a Social Act: Theology and Practice*, ed. Arthur Van Seters (Nashville: Abingdon Press, 1988), 85-91. Used by permission.

CHAPTER NINE

Thanksgiving, Mother's Day, and Days of Recognition

Preaching Grace through Civic Holidays

Sometimes you can tell more about where people are coming from by reading their bumpers stickers than by noting the state on their license plates. My attention was snagged recently by a red bumper sticker plastered prominently on the back of a late-model, no-nonsense sedan:

IT ISN'T SURPRISING AMERICA CAN'T FIND GOD—
WE'VE BANNED HIM FROM OUR SCHOOLS!

Prayer in school, the national flag in church—should we, or shouldn't we? Both issues are bones of contention for many who hold strong feelings about the mixing of politics and religion. While it is perhaps not very responsible, it is quite possible for preachers to ignore "church-state" relations from one week to the next, especially during certain seasons of the liturgical year. But there are days on which it is impossible to *avoid* such questions, even if the preacher decides to *ignore* them. What kind of sermon can address the themes of "secular" holidays? "No response" is not really an option, because even that answer sends a clear message.

The themes of some occasions—Memorial Day, Veterans Day, Independence Day, Labor Day, and Martin Luther King's Birthday, for example—have high potential for becoming politically partisan, charged, even volatile. Other occasions—Mother's Day, Father's Day, New Year's Day, "Founders' Day," or a city centennial celebration—seem relatively innocuous, unless someone is looking for a chance to grind an ax. Thanksgiving Day may be somewhere in the middle of this "hot button" spectrum.

There are several familiar poses that preachers tend to strike on such occasions:

- "It doesn't belong in the pulpit. The task of the sermon is to proclaim the Good News of Jesus Christ, not to focus on mothers, soldiers, pilgrims, or laborers." The sermon preached, therefore, becomes one more instance of religious business-as-usual.
- "The preacher needs to say something about this subject every once in a while, and this is the appointed day for making the appropriate nod." What follows, then, are a few well-chosen observations on the topic.
- "It's high time we took a significant stand!" Moral exhortations, analyses, injunctions, and platitudes then follow.
- "The Bible has a relevant word for all of us on this special day." The ensuing sermon is pieced together from some or all of the alternatives above, such as a Veterans Day sermon on "the whole armor of God" from Ephesians 6 talking about the importance of being prepared for "spiritual warfare" and implicating but not addressing the nation's military policies.

Once again, what we have to do as preachers is to find a way of preaching *through* these special days rather than *around, about,* or *at* them. What we usually look for when we sit down at the sermon preparation table with the scriptures and a civic celebration, I suspect, is *direct relevance.* At times it may well be there. We are more likely, however, to find something we are not hunting for. So rather than look for a topic-to-topic connection between scripture and civic celebration, we may do better being attentive to potential sparks between images, actions, and questions in scripture, and attitudes, feelings, tensions, or ideals that infuse the cultural holiday.

Another way to come at the sermon is to ask several questions of the text and the occasion:

- ∾ What seems to be the implicit *journeys* in the sacred texts and in the secular vision that the civic celebration symbolize?

- ∾ In what ways do these journeys seem to parallel and come into contact with each other? How do they question, critique, illuminate, and enrich one another?

But how does such a homiletical vision play itself out practically? Let's look at a couple of examples of how sermons on civic holidays might develop.

∾ *Mother's Day*

I have been asked to preach on the Sixth Sunday in Eastertide, which is also Mother's Day. The appointed texts from scripture are: Acts 17 (Paul's sermon before the philosophers of Athens); 1 Peter 3 (an encouragement to faithful suffering for the cause of Christ, and the exhortation to be ready, on demand, to give "a reason for the hope that lies within you"); and John 14 (Jesus' words to his disciples, in the wake of his imminent departure, that they must keep his love commandment and that he will not leave them orphaned, but will send them an Advocate whom the world will not be able to comprehend).

The setting for this sermon is a small, vital, multicultural, inner city parish that is currently a center for critically needed social services. Funding for parish operations, however, as well as for the social services, is in serious jeopardy because the economy is stagnant and the city government is in shambles. Wealthy churchgoers in the city, by and large, attend (and pledge) at other parishes. The highly competent, well-respected rector is away for the day. Although I am a somewhat familiar figure, having preached there previously on three occasions, I am still a guest in the pulpit. How should I preach?

I could speak about motherhood and the pressing concerns of mothers, making some quick connections between the gospel text and Mother's Day via Jesus' promise not to leave the disciples "orphaned." I could thunder about the actual abandonment of vulnerable mothers and children both by those who champion abortion on demand and by those who argue for "family values." Any such sermon strategies, however, especially in this setting, would have all the force of a dimestore kazoo.

I could ignore Mother's Day altogether, and wrestle with some rich and rigorous tensions between the scriptural texts and the social/congregational context. This would seem to have more homiletical promise; in addition, since it is an Episcopal church, there will not be an expectation (as there often is in other traditions) that mothers make it to center stage in the sermon of the day. Indeed, the expectation will probably be that I should practice homiletical avoidance.

Clearly, there is nothing to be gained by trying to force-fit several non-matching puzzle pieces into a single sermon. And yet, there are a number of splendid matriarchs in the parish, and a number of younger mothers, both married and single.

Is there, I wonder, a word from the Lord for them on this day? Is there a word from the Lord to the rest of us from or through them? With what cluster of images, ideas, or stories can I celebrate with them their life in God?

Suppose I played with a rough sermon plot that begins with the reading from Acts, and Paul's "apology" before the philosophers of Athens.

1) If I "offer you an apology," you probably think that I have done something wrong and am trying to make amends. "Apology," however, can mean something else. In his famous apology before the court of ancient Athens, Socrates makes no excuses and expresses no remorse. Rather, he sets forth a ringing defense of his quest for rational self-understanding among his fellow citizens. This is precisely the sort of "apology" that St. Paul is undertaking before his listeners on Mars Hill.

2) Paul wins few converts with his apology, which might make one think that his efforts are wasted. The author of 1 Peter, however, seems to think otherwise in the epistle reading for today, urging that all Christians prepare themselves to offer this kind of witness.

3) Such a defense sometimes takes the form of setting forth a sound conceptual argument, or of showing that objections to Christian belief are themselves invalid. But this strategy alone seldom "converts" an unbeliever. What is needed is something less abstract, something more tangible, more alive.

4) Often, however, we do not feel we have much to offer. We seem to lack all kinds of resources for setting forth a solid case—not just intellectual resources, but physical, emotional, and financial resources as well. How, after all, can we give the people of this community a "reason

to hope" when we do not even have the money to give them the medicine they need?

5) In the gospel reading, Jesus' disciples, too, felt that they were being left "high and dry" when Jesus told them of his impending death. Judging from the "orphan" language that Jesus uses in John's gospel, the disciples sound as if they feel like motherless children.

6) Yet Jesus promises them a continuation of nurturing love—which they will be able to sense more clearly as they live into it more deeply. He promises that they will experience the power of his love as though it were an advocate—not a corporate lawyer-type, but a strong mother who will stop at nothing to stand up for her own children.

7) The disciples eventually come to realize that, even though much of the rest of the world thinks they are crazy, they in fact have nothing to "apologize" for. The spirit of the risen Christ is their apology. It is an awesome, nurturing, "maternal logic" that flows to them and through them, a loving reason for being that enables them to enfold others in the same nurturing, "stand-up-for-you" kind of love that they themselves are experiencing.

8) How do you in this parish continue to do all that you do? To anyone who has not experienced the love of the "Mother-Advocate," what you all are about here seems like sheer madness. The answer you give to such incredulity is a real, live reason for the hope that is in you. You have courageously chosen not to leave this neighborhood orphaned. And God will not abandon you, but will be for you an apology of boundless love.

I make no pretense of this sermon sketch being finished, let alone a standard by which other sermons should be judged. Its value in this context is simply to show what can happen (often, as in this case, quite spontaneously) if the preacher will resist the urge to preach *around, about,* or *at* the civic holiday. The effect for me in this preliminary exercise of sermon shaping was to see more deeply what John's image of "Helper/Comforter/Advocate/Paraclete" might mean—which I would not have seen without the challenge of envisioning the text through the window of Mother's Day.

❧ *Thanksgiving Day*

You will find, I think, that the following Thanksgiving Day sermon avoids what it should avoid and includes what it should include with power and grace. It was preached to a southern congregation whose level of education, sense of tradition, and appreciation for history and national heritage are all very strong. The congregation includes leaders in economics and government, as well as military personnel, families, and retirees, all of whom are tempted to identify success and fulfillment with position and promotion. The preacher begins:

> People frequently think of the Thanksgiving festival as a time to do something called "counting their blessings." The assumption is that you won't mind your troubles so much if you reflect on what's going right. As though gratitude would help you to feel badly about feeling badly, so you'll feel better. That's bad psychology, because it's bad *theology*. It fails to get very deep into the mind because it fails to plumb the depths of the spirit.
>
> A firmer—and more biblical—grasp of Thanksgiving might be gained by reflecting on the *origins* of the holiday. And for its most significant origins, we ought not

to look to the dark days of 1621, but to the far darker days of 1863. That was when Abraham Lincoln set the day of the feast on the fourth Thursday of November, the day we have observed ever since. Prior to 1863, Thanksgiving festivals were held at different times in different places. It was Lincoln who fixed the date we still use.

That might seem strange, if one reflects for a moment on our national history. President Lincoln's own life was at a very low ebb in 1863. His political future looked bleak, to say the least. He knew that if he was defeated in the election of 1864, the Confederacy would gain its independence and the Union would be permanently split. His only significant victory to that point had been at Vicksburg, on the Mississippi River, but the effects of that victory were not yet being felt.

Many of the members of his own cabinet openly despised him, and joked about him in public. His wife had been investigated as a possible traitor—a process which Lincoln personally found to be bitterly wounding. In the face of such personal and national circumstances, Lincoln's call for a day of prayer would have made sense. But Thanksgiving? At a time like that? What must he have been thinking of?

President Lincoln must have discovered the same principle that St. Paul knew. At a similarly low point in his own life, Paul wrote to his friends: "Be anxious for nothing, but in everything by prayer and supplication *with thanksgiving* let your requests be made known to God." Paul was in prison when he wrote those words, fully expecting to be executed. He was at odds with the local Christian congregation. And yet, like Lincoln, he counseled thanksgiving—in the midst of great personal suffering.

Why? What did these two men understand? What they had learned was that in an emergency the one thing one needs most to remember is the first thing one tends to forget. Namely, the goodness of God....In the face of circumstances most of us will never be asked to endure, they had rediscovered God's goodness and mercy by giving thanks for it. Their giving of thanks was not an attempt at bribery. God does not require that. Instead, it focused their own spirits on the real sound of his voice in the midst of all the confusion and noise.

So we practice thanksgiving. Yearly, as Lincoln counsels; constantly, as St. Paul counsels. And as we offer ourselves in gratitude to God, we develop the same reflex that kept Lincoln joking through the war—and that kept Paul feisty and merry, as people can only be who have discovered that they can trust in the reliability of God.

In the discipline of giving thanks we have one more supreme example, of which we remind ourselves regularly. "In the night in which he was betrayed, he took bread; and when he had given thanks....Likewise, after supper, he took the cup, and when he had given thanks...." Were those acts of thanksgiving simply ritual? Hardly. That was not Jesus' style. He never did anything without being fully conscious and aware of its meaning. We are confronted with our Lord offering thanks for the very things that represent, for him and for us, the depths of unimaginable suffering. Why did Jesus give thanks that night? So that, as he entered into his ordeal, he might be able to clutch the memory of his Father's ultimate goodness. He took that memory to hell and back—until he was resurrected, to be forevermore the personal embodiment of God's goodness. Of God's reliability.

So, learning the reflex of Thanksgiving is no shallow trick we play upon our bad moods. It is a rule of life that locates us within a privileged order. An order that includes our nation's greatest president, our faith's greatest saint—and the Son of God, himself. And our thanksgiving is the gateway into the presence of our God, in the midst of any situation in which we find ourselves. As we give him thanks, he restores our knowledge of his goodness. And we realize that we are no longer alone, because he has joined us. Indeed, he has come to dwell in the midst of us.

Within a few hours of hearing this sermon on Thanksgiving morning, the congregation was confronted by a tragedy. Very early that morning, unknown to the preacher, one of the best-loved young women in the parish who had come home for Thanksgiving vacation was murdered in her own home. This sermon served as a centering point for the parish in its grief throughout the difficult days that followed. Who could have imagined that a sermon for a secular holiday would ever function as *that* kind of "grace-catcher"?

How then, to take on the task of preparing sermons for civic holidays?

Try to avoid:
- ignoring, perfunctorily acknowledging, or pontificating upon the "message" of the holiday;
- telling people what they ought to think, feel, or do on a day such as this;
- making superficial connections between scripture and civic celebrations that trivialize the meaning of both.

Try to include:

      ∾ a conversation among scripture, celebration, and congregation that helps listeners to hear the scripture and the celebration in fresher, deeper ways.

What I have not addressed in this chapter is the "hard stuff": racism on the birthday of Martin Luther King, Jr., the many sides of patriotism on Independence Day, the anguish of war on Memorial Day and Veterans Day. How does the preacher deal with the deep conflicts that can affect a congregation's experience of civil holidays? That question, actually, has more to do with the difficult circumstances surrounding the holiday than it does with the day itself. So we will defer that question, but not for long. For "special circumstances" is the primary focus in the next chapter, the final group of special occasion sermons that we will consider.

PART IV

Circumstances as Preaching Prisms

CHAPTER TEN

Social Crises and Theological Conflicts

Preaching Grace through Troubled Waters

"What makes this day different?" What interrupts the flow of business as usual and gives the preacher an occasion for shaping a sermon that is a distinctive "grace-catcher"? A special occasion is created when particular *persons* are engaged with an unusual set of circumstances on an appointed *day*. Sometimes it is the "person" element that is clearly most important: Marcia's wedding, Bruce's funeral, Wilma's baptism, Larry's ordination, the feast of Absalom Jones, Clare of Assisi, or Thomas Gallaudet. At other times, the most important element is the day itself—Mother's Day, Memorial Day, Maundy Thursday. It is either the *day* or the *person* that sets the definitive tone for many if not most of the special occasion services that we preach.

Sometimes, however, important events occur, questions and conflicts arise, or preaching conditions develop that are not closely associated with individual persons or particular days. These circumstances may come upon us suddenly and dramatically, as in the onset of the Gulf War. But usually these circumstances are ongoing, and at some point the preacher decides it is "high time" to address the situation. What kind of situations might these be?

Sometimes the special occasion is one of "troubled waters"—social conflict, theological disagreement, parish problem, or community crisis. Sometimes other factors come into play:

- ∾ *where* the sermon is delivered (a retreat, a weekday house eucharist);
- ∾ *when* it is being preached (in the middle of Lent or the end of Advent);
- ∾ *who* is preaching (a one-time pulpit guest, a former pastor);
- ∾ *for whom* the sermon is intended (a high school youth group, residents of a convalescent home, inmates of a prison).

There is a danger in including so many factors under the broad umbrella of "special circumstances," for every human event and every preaching event is in some respects unique. Every sermon is "special"—so what else is new? If "special occasion" includes everything imaginable, it might seem less than illuminating to talk about the subject at all. Yet there is a corresponding danger (and, I think, a more serious one) in defining special occasion preaching too narrowly, in restricting its focus to the "red letter days."

In those times in my life when I personally have been accorded special attention, the most positive, lasting impact has not come when others have put me on a pedestal or pillory, making a big deal about my major accomplishments or serious disasters. I have been more deeply changed when people in the normal course of daily life have observed and acknowledged something distinctive about me—whether healthy or destructive.

There is a rough parallel, I suspect, in preaching. What a pity it would be if preachers put all of their energy into pulling off extravaganzas about God's grace only when such sermons are expected, and never celebrated the distinctive shimmers of grace that constantly occur under more normal conditions! How much better for the eye of the preaching imagination to be constantly alert to whatever it might be that makes this day different! The grace of God needs to be experienced—and celebrated—as *special* at other times than those days on which it is "all dressed up."

Preaching in *special circumstances*, then, is the primary focus for this section of the book. This chapter will consider preaching in times marked by particular conflict, tension, or trauma. In the next chapter we will cover preaching with distinctive congregations that present their own challenges and possibilities. The final chapter will address occasions of extended preaching, such as a sermon series. It will be impossible, obviously, to treat any of these broad areas comprehensively; but perhaps I can at least suggest some of the factors to which, as preachers, we need to pay special attention.

∾ Preaching in the Midst of Tension and Struggle

Some people are adventurous types who seem to have a natural zest for troubleshooting. Most of the rest of us, I suspect, would just as soon live peacefully. We value tension in our lives the way we value salt and pepper: a little goes a long way—a bit of flavoring is fine, but a steady diet is something else. This reticence to wade into the center of tension is often manifested in the pulpit. Preachers tend to approach life's conflicts by way of cosmic abstraction: death and resurrection, sin and grace, materialism and spirituality, selfishness and sacrifice, temptation and resistance. Such preaching can easily convey the impression that the spiritual life is an existence substantially removed from the rough and tumble of the real world.

Insofar as real life tension *is* directly addressed in sermons, it is frequently reduced to a simple struggle between "where we know we really ought to be" on the one hand, and "where we always seem to find ourselves" on the other. "All the intractable problems of modern life are caused by our lack of faith." "If we would but trust in God...." Does this sound familiar? This is preaching *around* the troubled waters—if not by ignoring them outright, then surely by skirting in relative safety around the edges of the storm. It requires not only courage, but also homiletical discipline and imagination to steer into the middle—not in order to cry "Peace, peace, when there is no peace," but to help listeners get their spiritual bearings.

It is precisely in such dangerous places—where pontification does not reach and cannot help—that preaching is often most needed and most longed for. I have been talking with a fellow preacher whose hometown was recently hit by a tornado that did extensive damage to homes and to the church building. Attendance on the Sunday following, he said, was well above average. "You could see the question in their eyes: 'Is there a word from the Lord for us *today?*'"

Those with long experience in listening to sermons, however, often have low expectations in these preaching situations. There are some subjects, they are quite sure, the preacher "wouldn't touch with a ten-foot pole"—even though they profoundly wish he would. Then there are other listeners for whom certain topics are simply off-limits: "The pulpit is no place for dealing with abortion, domestic abuse, homosexuality, economic policy, or women's ordination!" Such sentiments can sometimes be expressed in ways that are more than a little intimidating. Another of my preaching colleagues, a woman, was recently invited to preach a Maundy

Thursday service at a small parish that was without a priest and had a history of intense conflict over the ordination of women. Her invitation came from the constituted parish leadership. After she had accepted the assignment, however, she heard indirectly that it would be bad for her reputation, and perhaps for her health, if she showed up to preach!

What is called for in the midst of social conflict, theological debate, community crisis, or highly charged parish issues is "prophetic preaching"—not pounding the pulpit or telling the future, but setting forth a discerning word that fosters a redemptive vision. Yet here, as on other special occasions, there will be the familiar temptations to preach *about* the storm by dispensing sociological, psychological, or theological information, or to preach *at* those who are caught up in the midst of the storm ("If we would but...")- The most natural homiletical response to a situation of troubled waters, in other words, is either to fix it or to forget it—whether the troubled waters involve a social dilemma, a theological debate, a parish difficulty, or a crisis precipitated by human agency or "act of God."

The urge to fix it or forget it are, after all, fundamental human instincts in the face of tension and conflict. The "forget it" response—also known as denial—is involved every time we succumb to the temptation to preach *around* the situation by ignoring it altogether or circumventing it with pious abstractions. If we are unable or unwilling to forget a troubled situation, then we try to fix it through increased knowledge and willpower. "If we know enough about the problem, we can figure out how to fix it. What we need here is more and better information." From that assumption proceeds a sermon *about*—statistics on hunger, abortion, or abuse, demographics on prison populations, data gleaned from historical-critical exegesis, insights uncovered from word studies of ancient languages, a summary of the stages of grief, some principle of healthy conflict management, a history of the interpretation of a problematic biblical text.

There is nothing wrong with information, of course. Broad, deep awareness and the ability to interpret information skillfully may be essential prerequisites for preaching through the situation with credibility and with integrity. But how helpful is information about troubled waters in stilling a storm? If debates over abortion or abuse, human freedom and the sovereignty of God, the right color for the sanctuary carpet or the meaning of the deaths of children in a school bus crash could be resolved by more knowledge, the "problem" might well be on its way toward resolution. But in most cases knowledge is not enough.

"The problem is not with the intellect; it is with the will." From that assumption flow sermons *at*—exhortations to picket, to pray, to patch up our differences, to trust in the face of tragedy we cannot understand, to cry and rage with righteous indignation, to work more energetically against sexual exploitation, to love our enemies, to love ourselves. These "willpower" sermons succeed in stilling the troubled waters about as effectively as their homiletical cousins, the "knowledge" sermons. The problem remains.

∿ *Preaching Through*

How do we develop a feel for what is involved in "preaching *through*"? Perhaps by reminding ourselves of a familiar account from Mark's gospel. When Jesus approaches his disciples, walking across the stormy sea, he brings along with him neither information nor exhortation. He brings, rather, a personal presence that does not so much "fix the problem" as it does mysteriously transcend and transfigure it. "Take heart, it is I," he says. "Do not be afraid." When at first the disciples see him, they scream in fear. What they see is a ghost—perhaps the very one responsible for kicking up the storm to begin with. And now it is headed straight for them! What is actually the advent of grace *initially* escalates the crisis. In the gospel story, the wind does not cease until *after* Jesus has gotten into the boat with the terrified disciples.

I wonder if preachers sometimes think it is their responsibility to speak the words that will calm the waters, rather than finding a way to talk about the tumult—the upheavals and crises in which the grace of God may already be approaching us, to our utter terror, through the very midst of the storm. This kind of speaking involves patiently waiting for, trying out, wrestling with, and fine-tuning those images, ideas, stories, and sermon plot lines that are clear and vivid, without seeking solutions. A sermon in troubled waters will try to lead its listeners to say "Oh, look!" rather than "That'll fix it!" Well-intentioned though we may be, we too easily fall into thinking that it is our job as preachers to still the storm. That is both a dangerous claim and an impossible burden. There is only One whose word the seas obey. Our job as preachers is to point to that One.

The "special circumstances" through which we may be called to preach are so numerous that no single book can hope to do them justice (to say nothing of a single chapter).[1] My concern here is to foster a broad homiletical vision. That vision could be stated succinctly: Preaching troubled waters sermons should not be marshaled to fix the problem, but are designed to invite listeners more deeply into the mysteries of finitude, brokenness, and grace. These are mysteries of which troubled waters are often only the symptoms.

First of all, it is very difficult in such preaching, if one goes into the center of the crisis or conflict (rather than denying or skirting it), to keep from polarizing strong opinions that arise from deep feelings. Though risk is involved, it is essential for the preacher to be both transparent and vulnerable, which is not at all the same as giving a piece of one's mind, or getting something off one's chest. Listeners can only be open to the advent of grace themselves if they are clearly oriented as to where the preacher is standing. A smoke screen of platitudes or abstractions is of no help.

Next, the issue—be it a controversial social policy or an intractable social problem, a bitterly contested community concern, a complex and emotionally charged theological conflict, or an unexpected disruption of community life—needs to be identified clearly in engaging and descriptive language. This requires paying special attention to the features that make it a conflict. The preacher will then seek to reframe the situation in the light of grace and awaken the imagination of the congregation to the opportunities for living into grace that would hardly have been conceivable apart from the conflict.

Clearly, this does not involve running away from thorny questions about race, sexual identity, economic justice, war, or biomedical ethics. Questions of doctrine or scriptural interpretation, personal or programmatic conflict in the parish, agonizing indecision and protracted suffering in crisis—all of these will have to be addressed at one time or another. There are times when the preacher will, after much prayer and careful reflection, find it necessary to preach an unpopular word. Such a hard word will be spoken, however, not from an exalted, privileged position, but from the midst of the congregation—the preacher sharing the stressful journey through the storm. The pulpit does not put the preacher "six feet above contradiction," but where all can see and hear clearly, the better to be able to watch and listen with the preacher for the word that comes both from within and beyond the conflict.

So preaching through troubled waters, as we have observed in several other contexts, requires shaping sermons that engage their listeners as participants in the process. The other dimension of "preaching *through*," which we have also noted at a number of points, is especially relevant here: using the scriptures and the situation as mutually illuminating. Fresh insight on a seemingly problematic text may well come by attending to it through the perspective of the very conflict that seems itself so intractable, while seeing a troubled situation through the window of a biblical text can evoke a similar revelation.

I remember the effort of a preacher who felt called upon to address the troubled waters of radical social and economic inequality. She did not offer any "fix it" solutions. She invited her listeners into a deeper understanding of Christian vocation by a fresh telling of the parable of the prodigal son. The result was not simply the application of a "timeless truth" to a current condition, but a fresh experience of both scripture and social circumstances, as each was brought into constructive dialogue with the other. She began as follows:

> If Jesus of Nazareth were to come among us today, and we wanted to see Him, we would probably have to look for him in a soup kitchen somewhere. We would find him sitting at a table in the middle of the hall, surrounded by street people who had come for food for their bodies, but found instead food for their souls.
>
> Imagine a young mother with several children, gaunt and pale; but now, the soup already consumed, their eyes would be riveted on Jesus, and a faint glimmer of hope discernible in the mother's eyes. A toothless old man, wearing a jacket several sizes too large, is sitting across from him, slumped back on his chair, but listening intently. These are people we seldom see in our churches. Where do they come from? Where do they live?
>
> To hear what Jesus is saying, we'll have to press closer. We want to listen, but we don't want to get too close. It's

not that we have anything against these people. Why should we? It's just that, well, when we go into the city for a movie and we see one of them rummaging through the garbage, we turn our eyes. It's embarrassing, but we aren't exactly sure what the embarrassment is about. And so we remain standing, wishing we could get Jesus to come to *our* church where it's so much more comfortable!

I think the setting of today's gospel reading is like this. Luke writes: "Now all the tax collectors and sinners were coming near to listen to him. And the Pharisees and the scribes were grumbling and saying, 'This fellow welcomes sinners and eats with them.'"

The preacher goes on to imagine Jesus telling the story of the prodigal son to the people in the soup kitchen, as he did so long ago in Jerusalem. She retells the story for her congregation—the younger son's return, the father's joy, the elder brother's refusal to come to the party. The father finally goes out to the elder brother in the fields and reassures him:

"Son, you are always with me, and all that is mine is yours." You see, our God is merciful, but He is also *just*. He will not take away what has been given. The younger son has been restored to full sonship, but as for material possessions—they have been squandered. The only way he can be restored to wealth is through his brother.

Jesus leaves the parable there. What do you think? Did the older brother go in and rejoice with the younger, or did he go home and refuse to face the prodigal who had wasted his own inheritance? It's a big question. For the older brother it is *the* question, for he too is lost. How will he ever "come to himself"? There are two options open to him: to go to the party or to leave and live apart. If he goes in and sees his brother, what will he say? What will

138

he do? It's all very awkward—the younger boy standing there at the punch bowl waiting...for what? The older brother doesn't like being out of control. He doesn't like feeling awkward. And he's perhaps afraid that if he once talks with the prodigal he might do something crazy, like get involved in the problem—perhaps help him get the lost wealth back.

You see, I believe that he's afraid of his own compassion! I think he's so afraid of his compassion that he won't go to the party. If that older brother will only go to the party, that very compassion which he fears will be the source of his "coming to *himself*"! When compassion is stirred in us, other feelings also come to life. But when compassion is denied, we are only half living. No wonder we are a society which looks for our pleasure in alcohol and drugs and anything that will numb us to the raw feelings we are suppressing.

All these years we've thought that what was demanded was our money. Money, we think, will take care of anything and everything. We write out a check and feel a little better about the starving people in Africa—at least until the next disaster gets our attention. And our collective giving certainly does a great deal of good in the world. But giving only money is not what the gospel is about. Jesus never once gave anyone money! He never gave anybody anything of a material nature, except for a little bread and fish, to show how far food will go when it is expanded by love.

Like the older brother, we are with God always. Everything He has is ours. God does not require that we give up anything. We're simply asked to call the father's other children "brother" and "sister" and enter into their suffering. In order to know and experience the fullness of God's love—and in order fully to "come to ourselves" the requirement is that we must *go to the party!*

There are many things about this sermon that are unique to the preacher's own voice, so any attempt to imitate her voice will not work. Are there, however, principles at work here that are transferable, that can help us ground the creative strategies of our own preaching voices? I think so. We can do what she has done when we preach through troubled waters:

Try to avoid:

- ᴔ platitudes and generalizations that suggest, "This is no problem";
- ᴔ pronouncements that "This can be fixed if we will but realize X, or do Y."

Try to include:

- ᴔ clear statements of the tension, conflict, or trouble in ways that invite listeners to experience the struggle viscerally;
- ᴔ provocative—but not imperious—suggestions as to how grace may be present in the storm, and how God may be leading the community into painful experience and costly choices;
- ᴔ treatment of the troubling circumstances as an exciting "adventure on the Sea of Galilee" in which God is providing resources along the way;
- ᴔ fresh insight on both the situation and scripture by interpreting each in light of the other;
- ᴔ clear indications of where you stand in relation to the congregation in the face of the situation.

Endnote

1. Many homiletical resources are available for addressing specific topics. Excellent, practical suggestions for preaching "hot topic" sermons are provided in Ronald J. Allen's *Preaching the Topical Sermon* (Louisville: Westminster/John Knox Press, 1992). Joseph R. Jeter offers deeply sensitive advice for preaching in the midst of crisis in his article "Crisis Preaching: Some Preliminary Reflections," published in the papers of the Academy of Homiletics, 1988, pages 200-213.

CHAPTER ELEVEN

Distinctive Congregations

Preaching Grace Through Special Conditions

To the attentive preacher, a religious or secular holiday, a rite of passage, a significant event in parish life, a critical social condition—any of these can provide the entry point for a fruitful approach to the perennial question, "What brings *us* together *today?*" But there are other points of entry as well. Sometimes what is "different" has to do more with the distinctive congregation gathered *on* an occasion, rather than with the occasion per se. The following questions might help the preacher to remember the circumstances that help set the context for a sermon:

- ∽ What is the size of the congregation—large, small, or somewhere in between?
- ∽ Is the congregation welcoming the preacher as a guest in the pulpit?
- ∽ Has the congregation gathered not for a Sunday celebration, but a weekday eucharist or prayer service?
- ∽ What is the make-up of the congregation—children, adolescents, parent, senior citizens, or all of the above?

It will seldom do, under such conditions, to make the "special" factor the explicit focus of the sermon, as in "What does God have to say to this small group?" or "I pray that what I say will meet your needs, even though I am a stranger to this congregation" or "Now, children (or septuagenarians)...." Rather, the principle of preaching *through* the occasion must be applied with even greater sensitivity. It simply does no good to preach *about* or *at* these conditions. And yet, as we have also seen, preaching *through* the occasion does not mean preaching *around* it—paying it no attention. In fact, precisely the opposite is the case, especially in this context. The more carefully we attend to the distinguishing features of the preaching situation, the more likely it is that we will be able effectively to preach *through* these features and touch the imagination of the people who have gathered to listen.

With that in mind, let's give some attention to each of the preaching conditions that we have just named.

℘ Large and Small Congregations

It is a very different experience to preach before hundreds of people in a large cathedral space than it is to share God's word with a small circle of friends who are gathered in someone's living room. The difference involves more than adjusting the volume of one's voice, the speed of one's delivery, and the size of one's gestures. In both settings, of course, the preacher would like to engender a sense of sacred conversation, drawing the participants deeply into dialogue with God's word. In both settings, the preacher will strive for a sense of immediacy and presence: "I felt that she really knew us! She was talking to us right where we are!"

How that sense of connection can best be created will differ markedly from one physical space to the other, even though it may not always be easy to specify just what the preacher must do to bring it about. Two observations may help us in trying to get at the difference between addressing a large congregation and a small one, a difference that is difficult to translate into specific sermon strategies or techniques. In a small group, the preacher is like a chamber music ensemble; in a large group, she is a full orchestra. Intensity, phrasing, variation in tempo and mood—all of these are involved in making both kinds of homiletical music. The difference has to do with the degree of richness, with how elaborate the verbal orchestration, regardless of how "formal" or "informal" the language may be.

I will never forget a sermon that as a newly ordained priest I wrote and preached, word for word, to a congregation consisting of three people. It just didn't fit. Not only did my reading of the sermon text seem to isolate me from my fellow worshipers, but the very conceptual structures and verbal turns of phrase that might have engaged a larger audience, in this tiny group made it sound as if I were "putting on airs" and talking to no one in particular.

That leads to the second observation. A relatively small congregation is approached most effectively if the preacher connects with each participant in some way as an individual: with eye contact, at least, perhaps even with personal reference or address, if the participants are known to the preacher. In a relatively large congregation, on the other hand, the most effective sermon usually speaks to and for the group as a whole.

∾ Preaching as a Pulpit Guest

It is a very different thing for a preacher to step into the pulpit of his or her own congregation than into an unfamiliar pulpit. Here too, the most significant differences are not the ones that immediately meet the eye, such as the shape, size, or placement of the pulpit (if there is a pulpit at all); whether it can accommodate two stacks of letter-size paper or only a set of index cards; whether the acoustics in the room are "live" or "dead"; whether the architecture of the worship space is more compatible with the theology of Geneva or of Rome. To preach as a guest, wherever one is, is to preach in a very different space than to preach "at home."

Either one can be a graceful place in which to stand, if the preacher takes heed to where he or she is standing. Preaching in one's own church is less anxiety-producing for most, but the visiting preacher can channel the extra adrenaline to good advantage. Familiarity with a congregation gives the preacher more to build upon, but also more to overcome—either in terms of comfort or resistance on the part of the congregation. While familiar preaching patterns can make it easier for a congregation to follow the sermon, familiarity can also breed inattention, if not contempt. Either the home preacher or the home congregation may be in a rut, with patterns of speaking or listening unconsciously ingrained.

The resident preacher has more right than a guest preacher to deal with particular circumstances that are troubling the community—and also more responsibility. Facing the same crowd week after week also has a way of keeping preachers honest. Visiting preachers may not be listened to as closely or heard as well because their voices (at many levels) are strange to the ears of the congregation. And yet, in a single sermon, a visiting preacher may be the catalyst for a significant shift in the congregation's thinking in ways that the local preacher had tried to do in vain countless times, in all sorts of different ways. Fresh voices in the pulpit can be a very good thing.

To come as a guest preacher is also to offer a possibility of connection between the local congregation and the wider church. I once preached in a parish on a Sunday when a well-beloved rector was announcing his resignation in order to accept another call. It seemed, at first, wrong for me even to be there, let alone to preach; this was, after all, a "family" occasion. But afterward my colleague said that were he ever in the situation again, he would do the same. Having a guest preacher on that day enabled him to focus his emotional energy on the leave-taking announcement, while the congregation could experience firsthand that the proclamation of the gospel was not dependent on any one familiar preacher.

The very differences of style, experience, approach, and conviction that make a guest preacher sound somewhat alien are, in fact, the peculiar treasures that he or she will bring to the preaching space. If guest preachers know their own preaching voices well, and share their gifts without false humility, they will do the congregation and the local preacher a great service. Yet a guest in the pulpit cannot simply rely on piqued curiosity in the presence of novelty. He needs to do everything possible ahead of time to find out what is distinctive about the new preaching space. Even if the congregation is polite, or particularly receptive, a sermon from a guest that sounds like "to whom it may concern" will squander a significant opportunity. "I really don't know these people" is no excuse. This principle applies even if the sermon is a full manuscript prepared in advance and delivered without a word's deviation. Preaching places are different, and those differences need to be honored as much as possible.

ᑐ *Weekday Preaching*

Regardless of the size of the congregation or the worship space, the "full dress" presentation we do for the principal celebration on a Sunday is very different from how we prepare for weekday services (unless they celebrate one of the special events we have been considering in the last several chapters). This does not mean that what goes on at weekday celebrations is less important. Indeed, for some people at certain points in their lives, weekday services may be considerably more important. While both Sunday and weekday preaching can give perspective to our lives, the Sunday celebration is a "day of rest," a withdrawal from business as usual in order to reflect, as a fully gathered Christian community, upon our lives before God. The weekday worship event is a briefer pause "to get our bearings." The weekday homily is not the place to develop a highly complex sermon plot; sermons for such days need to be more simply focused. Simply, but sharply—the weekday homily is not a place for aimless wandering.

Again, a comparison may be helpful. The Sunday sermon is painting in oils or acrylics. The weekday preaching event looks more like a simple watercolor, a line drawing, or even a charcoal sketch. The genres are different; one is not inherently "better" than the other. This difference presents the preacher with some freedoms that are less appropriate to the "heavier" medium. Let me suggest some weekday homiletical possibilities.

- ∾ While it is true that using one's own experience in sermons can function as an idol rather than an icon for hearers, there is probably more latitude for *personal reference* in a weekday homily.
- ∾ The weekday homily is a particularly good place to develop brief *character sketches* of personalities from scripture or church history (assuming that the homilist is preaching *through* and not *about*).
- ∾ There is more room in the weekday homily for *catechesis* and for indepth reflection on a specific *topic* (as distinct from a broader kerygmatic focus of Sunday preaching).

∾ The midweek service, especially if it is connected with a regular study or discussion program, may be a good place to "plant seeds" concerning innovative, practical *strategies for mission and social justice.*

∾ The smaller, more informal setting of the weekday service may offer more room for dealing with *theological controversy* in the homily by sowing the seeds for ensuing dialogue: "Does it make sense, do you think, to see the matter like this...?"

∾ While a *dialogue sermon* can be a risky strategy for Sunday morning, it may have a place in the more intimate homiletical space of the weekday setting, where the preacher may be able to incorporate more explicitly the ongoing concerns of regular participants (if they know and trust one another).

∾ The intimacy of the weekday service can make it an especially appropriate place for a *healing service.* For those in particular physical, emotional, and or spiritual need, there is the possibility of support from a gathered spiritual community apart from the Sunday morning congregation (where this special liturgical focus might undermine the primacy of baptism and the eucharist).

Preparation for weekday preaching is necessarily less expansive and more focused. When practiced well by the conscientious preacher, it can be a stimulating complement to the process of preparation for Sunday sermons and a vital element in a developing preaching life. The sermon in such a setting shapes an experience markedly different from its Sunday counterpart, one that can be a distinctive means of grace for those who share in it.

∾ *Preaching to Different Age Groups*

I shall never forget one particular Sunday, the day of the sermon from—well, it certainly did not feel like it was from heaven. Our parish was in the midst of a massive physical renovation project. The pews had been removed and the tattered old carpet had been ripped up. The new carpet had not been delivered when promised. Setting the pews in place for the coming Sunday service was not an option—when not bolted to the floor, they had a pronounced tendency to tip over. Aluminum folding chairs were imported for the day. The acoustics were definitely going to be "live" for the service. There were in our congregation four families, each of which had four children, all of whom were under the age of four. None of these families were regular attenders; no two of the families had ever showed up on the same Sunday. I do not need to tell you how many came to church on this particular Lenten Sunday. Suffice it to say that a critical mass of, by turns, cheerful, fretful, tempestuous tiny tots radically transformed an already altered sermon space!

The sermon I had planned for the morning was a highly complex dialogical argument. The text was from Romans, and I had constructed a theological masterpiece on "law and grace" which, I was quite sure, would win me high marks from Martin Luther and St. Paul. Perhaps it did. If so, I never heard from them—maybe because neither Martin nor Paul could hear what I was trying to say, either. Never have I encountered so much pandemonium in such a contained space in such a short period of time (which felt, for all the world, as though it went on for hours). I would have been far better advised simply to lead the congregation in the singing of "Jesus Loves Me" and proceed to a celebration of the eucharist.

Children make a difference to the preacher. The more important question is, of course, by the grace of God, how can the preacher make a difference to *them?* And children are not the only "special interest group" that come to church. My own sense of the average—dare I say it, "normal"—parishioner was more gently but even more utterly shattered for me one Sunday when I had the privilege of preaching to a Florida retirement community congregation where the median age was easily seventy-five. I have never been so lovingly but powerfully convicted of my utterly insular vision as I was when, after the sermon, I administered communion to scores of patient, wrinkled hands. I must confess I do not remember what or how I preached on that occasion; the lingering impression, however, is of a "to whom it may concern" sermon in which both the "to whom" and the "concern" were powerfully, albeit unconsciously, shaped by my own "mid-forties" experience.

C. S. Lewis once declared that an articulation of the gospel that is both substantive and intelligible to a six-year-old should be required of any candidate for ordination. If memory serves, he also said that in speaking with children one should restrict the range of one's concepts and language, yet still address them face-to-face (rather than from above) with respect to all one actually discussed. That is, I think, a practical way of translating Paul's declared intention to "be all things to all people" in bearing witness to God's love. It is also a principle with transfer value, regardless of the special constituency of a congregation.

∾ Preaching Through

Once the process of reflection on the diversity of our listeners has begun, there is no place it can legitimately end. The issue is: how can people who stream toward the mountain of the Lord from the west, east, north, and south, who differ in race, gender, age, and social circumstance, receive in the sermon a reprise of Pentecost, hearing in his or her own language the mighty works of God? It is obviously far beyond the scope of this book to fill in the details of the homiletical truism that different types of people need to be preached among differently—let alone to wrestle significantly with the challenge of convening for all of them a communal banquet rather than a "serve yourself" buffet. The ideal is not an "equal time" rule, but a commitment to taking the particularities of the human condition seriously in practical ways.

That is probably a good place, not to conclude, but to move to something more concrete. Since the range of suggestions in this chapter has been so wide, it does not seem particularly fruitful to end with a "try to avoid/try to include" list or to reflect on specific ways one can preach *around, about,* or *at* these circumstances. By this point, you will doubtless be able to flesh out the specifics with more imagination than I can. One thing is surely clear: preaching *through* any or all of these factors seldom, if ever, involves explicitly *referring to* them in the sermon itself.

As a stimulus to your own creativity, here are two sermons whose treatment of scripture and manner of presentation are profoundly shaped by the special homiletical conditions under which they were delivered. Both preach *to* by preaching not *about* or *at,* but *through* the sermon space.

The first takes a highly abstract epistle text from Romans and shapes it with vivid imagery for a weekday healing service attended by adults with a fair degree of theological sophistication. That training does not mitigate the need for healing; hence the preacher's careful development of the opening image. Part of "healing," however, involves encountering a new framework of understanding. Notice how this takes place in the interweaving of the experience of the preacher, the special needs of the congregation, and the fresh look at the scripture text.

Several years ago, my husband and I began organic gardening. What dreams we had for our garden! We poured over the Burpee seed catalog and fantasized about the fruits of our labors. We ordered back copies of *Organic Gardening* magazine, armed ourselves with the newest variety of gardening implements, and were ready to sow. Or so we thought. As it turned out, we were totally unprepared for the vicissitudes of Virginia clay.

Red, sticky, Virginia clay. If it is too dry, it forms a hard crust that prevents tender young seedlings from breaking through. If it is too wet, clay holds groundwater so efficiently that the seeds rot or drown. The first year was a disaster. Most of our plants never broke the dry ground. The mint and the zucchini did emerge, only to drown in our enthusiastic irrigation. We bought all of our vegetables at the market that year.

But hope springs eternal in the gardener's heart. To remedy the clay problem, we began composting. Every day we collected our discarded vegetable peelings, fruits that no longer met the *Good Housekeeping* Seal of Approval, eggshells, coffee grounds, and sawdust from the guinea pig's cage. We took the mixture to the corner of our yard near the garden and added it to the compost pile. At first, the compost pile was just a sorry looking pile of trash. For a long time there was no apparent change. We just kept adding more junk to the pile. Occasionally we dug around it with a pitchfork, but that was an unpleasant job. So we waited.

Composting is a slow process. It would be great if we could throw a banana peel directly on the zucchini or an eggshell on the mint. But it doesn't work that way. For it is in the waiting that the transformation occurs. Deep inside that pile of useless discards, something begins to happen. Slowly and almost imperceptibly, the garbage begins turning into something useful.

Today's lesson reminds me of our garden and the composting process. Each of us is faced with an assorted pile of suffering—illness, disappointment, loneliness, and grief. Each pile is different. Sometimes we add to the pile we are faced with. Our attempts to dig around in it and sort it out are unpleasant. So we wait. But as we wait, something begins to happen. We discover that God's love, his mercy and his grace have been present all along, and we begin to see glimpses of hope in the midst of our suffering. We find God's love in the smile of a friend. We find God's mercy in the healing of a relationship, and we find God's grace in each new dawn.

St. Paul tells us in today's lesson: "Suffering produces endurance, and endurance produces character, and character produces hope, and hope does not disappoint us, because God's love has been poured into our hearts through the Holy Spirit which has been given to us." Hope does not disappoint us. Hope is not about things turning out the way we want them to. Hope is as much about the past as it is about the future. Hope remembers. Hope remembers the rainbow after the flood. Hope remembers the barren womb of a ninety-year-old woman giving life to the promise of Israel. And hope remembers the angel at the empty tomb announcing, "He is not here. He is risen."

By remembering the transforming power of God's love, hope stakes a claim in the healing promise of God's future. Hope is about looking back on our own useless pile of suffering and discovering that God was there all along, transforming our commonplace experiences into occasions of grace. Through the power of God's love, our own unique mixtures of circumstantial compost provide the spiritual nourishment we need to grow strong and straight, faces lifted toward the Son.

The second sermon was offered to a congregation of high school students at a religious boarding school. The families who send their children there are successful and affluent. Peer pressure to conform is, of course, as strong as parental pressure to achieve. Chapel is required, with seating sections assigned. The text of the psalm could sound to adolescent ears as though God is one more pressure—a cosmic, frowning, Big Brother to cower before or rebel against. But listen to how this preacher takes this congregation through this text.

> The first time I laid eyes on Kim Coleman my heart skipped a beat. I knew immediately that she was the one for me. Two small things kept us from settling down, getting married, and starting a family right away. For one thing, Kim Coleman didn't know that I existed. For another, we were both in the first grade. Now, I don't recall thinking that the first grade part was a big problem, and I had a plan to capture her attention—which I immediately put into action. When I was six years old, I spoke the words that I was sure every girl wanted to hear. I told Kim Coleman that I was a professional song writer, and that my parents let me drink coffee.
>
> I think she must have been pretty impressed, because after that we were inseparable. We spent every recess playing on the swings together. When our teacher lined us up in two lunch lines—girls and boys—Kim Coleman would give "cuts" to as many girls as it took to get even with my place in the boys' line. We sat together during lunch and story time. Once she even held my hand for a

minute that seemed like an hour. I didn't like it very
much, but I liked the idea of it a lot.

Everything was going along just great. I was a
six-year-old coffee-drinking songwriter, and Kim
Coleman was my groupie. That is until the day she asked
me if I would bring one of my songs to school so that she
could look at it. This...was a problem. I barely knew how
to write my first name, and she wanted to check out one
of my musical compositions. I was in trouble. I was sure
that I would be found out, and Kim Coleman wouldn't
love me anymore. I worried my six-year-old self sick. I
was so desperate, I even considered telling her the truth.
Then it occurred to me that I could find a song that she
had not heard before.

That night, after everyone in our house was sleeping, I
tiptoed into the den and opened the top of the old piano
bench. I grabbed the first piece of sheet music I saw and
ran to the bathroom. Behind the locked door, I tried to
sound out the title of the song that was printed on the
sheet. "O Wh-wh-wh-en—When—the S-s-s-ai-ai-n-t-s—
Saints—Come Mar-mar-ching—Marching In. O When
the Saints Come Marching In."

"Jackpot!" I thought. "*Nobody's* ever heard of this
song!" And I ripped the name of the composer off the
bottom. The next day I brought "my" song into Mrs.
Gerwick's first-grade class. On the playground I gave it to
Kim Coleman. She glanced at it and skipped off toward
the monkey bars. As far as I could tell, she bought it.

But a strange thing happened after that. Kim
Coleman and I grew apart. To tell the truth, from that
day on, I avoided her like the plague. I was scared to
death that she was going to ask me about "O When the
Saints Come Marching In," or to make me prove that I
drank coffee. I didn't sit with her in the classroom, and

on the playground I ran away from her. After two romantic weeks, and two very bad days, the handwriting was on the wall: Kim Coleman and I had irreconcilable differences.

When we pray Psalm 139 together, as we did today, we each speak directly to God: "O Lord, you have searched me and known me. You know my thoughts and my ways. Even before a word is on my tongue, O Lord, you know it completely. Lord, even before I told Kim Coleman that I was a coffee-drinking songwriter, you began to feel me running away from her, from my true self, and from you, God."

In truth, we are all runaways—every one of us. We want others to respect us, to accept us, and to love us. Yet we rarely meet each other honestly—face to face. We wear phony masks that accentuate the positive and bury the negative. We masquerade as an intellectual or athletic person, a patient teacher or a gifted student, a liberal or a conservative, a spiritual person or a real rebel. We've got an image. And every time we put on the mask, we run away from the person God made us to be.

And when it works, when someone falls in love with our mask, what then? If someone loves me in my Mr. Self-Assured mask, I can never reveal that I get scared, too. If someone falls in love with your sense of style, or your physical beauty, you can never tell them that sometimes you feel foolish or so damn ugly. Our phony masks leave us to deal with our inner struggles alone. Deep down, the flaws and fears that we've buried alive eat at us: "Nobody would love me if they *really* knew me. If they knew how dishonest, perverted, and hypocritical I can be at times, if they only knew the lust, the anger, the frustration, the doubt I sometimes feel—nobody would even look at me.

But God says: "STOP!"

"I have searched you and known you. I know your thoughts and your ways. Even before a word is on your tongue, I know it completely." We can't hide anything from God and we don't need to. We need only to turn... to turn to Jesus—sorry for the sins we foolishly try to hide. In Jesus, God meets us as a real person—face to face. "In Jesus, I was poor," says God. "In Jesus, I felt lonely and scared like you do. In Jesus, I suffered a painful death and rose again." Our sins are already forgiven. God says, "I've searched you out and known you and there is nothing to hide."

Tonight, when you turn off your light, give yourself a break. If you think you're the greatest, you're wrong. If you think you're the worst, you're wrong. But of this you can be sure: your life is in the hands of God, who knows you inside and out, good and bad, and he loves you just as you are. Whatever you think or don't think about God, tonight when your head hits the pillow, simply close your eyes and say to God silently in your heart, "I will not run away from you." Whatever you believe—just say it: "God, I will not run away from you." Then just be still and listen.

The day after this sermon was delivered, a senior administrator approached the preacher. "One of the students told me that he did what you told him when he went to bed last night," he said. "That makes two of us." When a sermon is effectively focused with artistry for one set of "special circumstances," it may well speak to others also.

CHAPTER TWELVE

Retreats, Preaching Missions, and Liturgical Seasons

Preaching Grace through the Faith Journey

Throughout this book we have been talking about preaching grace on special occasions. As we turn now to preaching at retreats, extended missions, and sermons that carry a theme through a liturgical season we suddenly seem to be switching gears, from preaching on single occasions to preaching several sermons over extended periods of time. You are entitled to wonder: "Isn't such a shift contrary to the entire thrust of this book?" Why prepare a series of sermons for a preaching mission or a set of meditations for a time of retreat or a collection of homilies focusing on a single seasonal theme? Because theologically, at least, there is more to an "occasion" than what can be administered in a single dose. There is, in fact, more to any human action than what can be captured in the moment. Actions are never discrete points in time; rather, they are always *processes*. The acts of God are not "zaps," even though the "ah ha!" of human recognition may seem to happen all at once.

Paul's conversion is often depicted as a dramatic Damascus Road experience, but it was, in fact, a *journey* that began before Jerusalem and ended far beyond Damascus. As Luke describes it in the book of Acts, the journey began with someone named Saul participating in the stoning of Stephen, and concluded with the recovery of Saul's sight at the hands of Ananias. But these are only the two arbitrary points at which the reader enters and leaves this story of God's graceful transforming action in the life of Saul, who eventually becomes known as Paul. These boundaries on Paul's conversion experience do not really tell the whole story: in the scriptural record the story continues without interruption through Saul's initial attempts at gospel proclamation in the synagogues of Damascus, the plot to assassinate him, his escape with the aid of the very followers of Jesus whom he had come to squelch, his return to Jerusalem, his endorsement by Barnabas, and his escape to Tarsus from a second attempt on his life. Where, in all of this, did Saul's conversion "take"? It would be *truly* arbitrary to identify the "special occasion" of Saul/Paul's conversion with the sudden light that blinded him in the midst of his geographical and spiritual journey, or the laying on of hands by Ananias, or his endorsement by Barnabas.

All of this suggests that, important though single sermons may be at particular points in one's spiritual life, it is essential to see these sermons as part of a homiletical trajectory. Simply put, a single sermon delivered upon the occasion of a wedding, funeral, baptism, Memorial Day, or Christmas Eve is not likely in and of itself to have a lasting, life-changing impact. It is important for preachers to remember this, especially in light of the fact that everything in our culture— from "Sesame Street" to MTV—conspires to produce in all of us a "sound-bite consciousness." Meaning is given in the instant. It fades as quickly as it flashes, to be replaced by the next burst of images or bits of information.

Shaping a connected set of sermons for a preaching mission or liturgical season or weaving an integrated fabric of meditations for a retreat gives both preachers and listeners an opportunity to broaden and deepen their understanding of a "special occasion." Preaching missions, retreats, and liturgical seasons are clearly framed homiletical "episodes" that invite significant reorientation and fresh perspective. The adventurous, "on the road" quality of a good individual preaching event can be given more expansive space without sacrificing the sharp focus of a single theme.

∾ *Preaching Missions*

The sermons of a preaching mission are to the individual occasional sermon what the novella is to the short story: the experience may not be as concentrated, but the impact may be more profound. The preaching mission—a series of sermons on a single theme, delivered at one time and place—provides a particularly effective opportunity for deep cognitive reflection. Subjects that are too extensive, complex, or controversial for effective treatment in a single sermon can be given breathing room in such a setting. Individual sermons in the series can each have their own integrity, but be crafted as though they were chapters or sections within the whole.

Through a series of clearly articulated moves, the listeners' theological reflection can be stimulated and shaped through a careful sequence of ideas. The strategy for these concepts, ideally, will be dialogical, rather than didactic. The preacher here is not trying to cover more points, provide more evidence, or give more illustrations than a single sermon will bear, but is trying to deepen or redirect theological reflection by means of fuller articulation and argument. In a time when the questions and content of Christian faith are widely given superficial, even glib treatment, the preaching mission can invite its listeners of all levels to love God with their minds as well as their wills and their feelings.

While it is important for the sermons in a preaching series to allow room for reflective work, this objective is likely to be achieved more effectively if each sermon unfolds with precision, with the intellectual energy that builds significant momentum. Each of the sermons in the series will manifest its own clear *telos,* its "track" of connected, unfolding ideas. The line of sight can shift from sermon to sermon, as long as each segment of the series is held in dramatic tension with the others. A preaching series does not have to be an extended religious monologue with a single focus: it can be an exciting theological excursion, ending in a new and exciting spiritual place.

∽ Retreats

Retreats provide space for reflection as well, but usually of a different kind. They allow greater room than normally afforded in a preaching mission for meandering, musing, and contemplating—in short, for holy forms of play. Like the preaching mission, the retreat intends to foster fresh vision and new perspective, but it does so more with *soft* focus than with *sharp* focus. A soft focus, however, does not mean that the leader's meditations can be fuzzy.

The retreat is to the preaching mission what poetry is to prose. As anyone who has ever seriously tried it can readily testify, writing poetry is highly disciplined, exacting, even tedious work. Robert Frost's "Two Roads Diverged in a Yellow Wood" is comprised entirely of simple words and uncomplicated phrases. I strongly suspect that it was not, however, simply tossed off by the poet in a few minutes of his spare time. "I took the road less traveled by," the poem concludes, "and that has made all the difference." It is precisely because the final line is shaped with such elegant, uncomplicated clarity that the same words are able to send different listeners off in different, equally fruitful directions (and even send the same listener into different places simultaneously).

The same cultural factors that make careful theological analysis difficult also war against the quiet, open space necessary for contemplation and the creative exercise of spiritual imagination. A retreat, like a several beat rest in music, is not "dead time" or "down time." It is time that centers, in which our scattered energies are reintegrated and redirected.

While it is true elsewhere in preaching, it is especially true in retreat meditations that the function of the spoken word is not to *fill* space, but rather to *shape* space. If preaching missions need a *telos*—an arrow shot on a specific trajectory with deliberate aim toward a goal of communal reflection—retreat meditations need to shape a distinctive *ethos*—an environment conducive to the needs of individual participants for open-ended exploration. The fruits of such exploration may be openly shared in the community of retreatants, but only by invitation, never upon command.

It might seem as though the leader should give little, if any, direction in each meditation or over the course of the retreat. Perhaps the retreat leader should simply toss out some images and ideas as "food for thought." But this is not so. Good retreats are never forced marches, but neither are they aimless wanderings. The pace is slower, the parameters far broader, the agenda less fixed. But if preachers are asked to *lead* a retreat, then some sort of leadership is indeed required. (There is a place for undirected retreats, but preachers have no role, as such, to play in them.) The participants may well end up going in different directions from those the leader has planned, and that is probably as it should be. But the Spirit will find it easier to lead individual retreatants down roads "less traveled by" if the retreat leader has a territorial map clearly in mind.

⌒ *The Liturgical Seasons*

I said earlier that the sermons of a preaching mission are to a single special occasion sermon what the novella is to the short story. You can guess where I want to take that line of imaging: the sermons of a liturgical season are to the sermons of a preaching mission or the meditations of a retreat what the novel is to the novella. If the occasion of St. Paul's conversion has no fixed beginning or ending, neither do seasonal sermons that intend to foster conversion in their listeners over the course of several weeks.

If a single occasional sermon is "preaching punctuation" and preaching missions and retreats are "preaching phrases," then seasonal preaching could be understood as "preaching paragraphs" in an ongoing, unfolding adventure story. Many preachers simply go from Sunday to Sunday, preaching *around*, *about*, or *at* the scripture texts for the day or the issues they think need addressing. But what if preachers preached *through* the dynamic shapes made possible by the seasons of Advent, Christmas, Epiphany, Lent, and Easter? What an engaging experience of grace their congregations might have!

The "sound-bite consciousness" of which we spoke earlier tends to infect preachers without their even recognizing it. The irony of this is that, in such a climate, the single special occasion sermon is likely to be both undertaken and experienced as this week's "one-day only" sale at the local variety story, or tonight's television "special." In other words, as so many minor variations on homiletical business as usual. "High time" preaching is not likely to do its particular work unless there is a constant, systematic attempt on the part of the preacher to create a sense of *kairos* by giving broad, episodic shape to the experience of the faith community. That is a very different approach to preaching from one which, with monotonous regularity, seeks to convince jaded listeners that "today we are going to do something different."

Preaching that fosters a sense of *kairos* cannot be undertaken in a liturgical vacuum. The critical themes of preparation, gift, witness, repentance, death and resurrection, and Spirit-led growth are embodied in faith journey episodes dramatized through the liturgical seasons of the church year. What a pity if the preacher plods through the year, all but oblivious to the distinctive rhythms inherent in these extended but still discrete "occasions"! When people come to church they need to hear more than familiar words: they need to reconnect with a coherent, clearly directed journey of grace. Preaching through the liturgical seasons can shape a space that no other liturgical element, educational program, mission project, growth group, or church social calendar can provide.

How does one prepare to preach seasonally? Not by describing "the seasons of the church year" or talking about "the liturgical colors on the altar today," or quoting "the collect for this, the third Sunday after the Epiphany" in one's sermons—preaching *about*. Nor by exhortations to live out the Easter imperative or undertake the disciplines of Lent—preaching *at*. Rather, the preacher shapes an unfolding series of sermons, each plotted in relation to the others—that is, by preaching *through* the season. Of course, the sermon six weeks from now cannot (and should not) be prepared ahead, put on the shelf, and then simply pulled down on Sunday morning. There must be freedom and flexibility as well as continuity to allow not only for the unexpected happenings, but also for the Spirit-led conversation that develops from one sermon to the next. You can count on it: such conversation, vigorous and vital, *will* occur—*if* the sermon preparation for each succeeding week does not start from scratch.

Reading through all of the lessons for a season *in advance* and *as a whole* is a must. Making rough notes as to images, actions, issues, and arguments that appear in each of the lessons is of critical importance. Some preachers find constructing a diagram or "flow chart" for each season tracing the themes and actions of the lessons can be an invaluable asset. The additional time it takes to do this preparation is saved many times over in the course of a preaching season. A momentum is created that is far more efficient than the energy it takes to shut down the sermon engine at the end of every week and cold start it again—after avoiding the prospect of cranking it up yet once more as long as possible. And in addition to being more efficient, this pattern of sermon preparation is much more fun!

If you are the only preacher for a congregation, this process of seasonal preparation will allow each new sermon to resonate with the sermon you have just preached, as well as those you will be preaching some weeks down the road. If you share the preaching responsibilities in a parish church with others, seasonal preaching preparation provides a wonderful opportunity to work on your preaching as a team of homiletical colleagues. In either case, you may well want to form such a team from among preachers in neighboring churches, or even on the Internet.

In preaching *through* the liturgical seasons you need not constantly speak of Advent, Lent, or Easter; indeed, you best *not* do so. But you need constantly to be asking yourself, your preaching colleagues, members of your congregation, and anybody else with whom you can strike up a conversation: "What is God's word of grace to us in this situation, in these scriptures, *in the light of this season?* Where is the Spirit taking us in relation to where we have just been? Where are we going as we move through this liturgical season?" Even asking the questions in your seasonal preparations can make a difference, a difference not so much explicitly recognized as tacitly sensed and instinctively responded to by those who hear you preach.

These suggestions are not intended as a step-by-step manual, but more like an unsophisticated scout compass. More important than that, however, is the suggestion that "special occasion preaching" need not, and indeed ought not to be defined exclusively in terms of single sermons. It is much more likely that appropriately crafted single special occasion sermons will be "grace-catchers" in the moment if they are supplemented by a much broader vision of occasional preaching. The ongoing experience of grace to be found in seasonal preaching—as in the series of sermons and meditations for preaching missions and retreats—is closely connected to the meaning of sacraments. And that is the focus to which I turn next in the conclusion.

What Makes an Occasion Special?

Every morning just before daybreak, wrote G. K. Chesterton, God says to the sun: "Do it again!" That may sound quaint, superstitious, or just plain silly. Any God most of us can manage to believe in presumably has better ways to begin the day than by issuing wake-up calls to the sun. Yet Chesterton's line is a vivid way of affirming a fundamental conviction of our faith tradition: that God "upholds all things by the word of his power"—that God is, at all points, intimately engaged with the affairs of the world.

The claim can be misconstrued, of course. God may well have more important things to do than to find me a parking place when I am late for a meeting, especially if that involves giving me preferential treatment over fifteen other drivers. For the Christian, however, an "act of God" is not merely legal terminology tucked away in the escape clauses of insurance policies. Nor is it the bizarre and arbitrary intrusion of a *deus ex machina*. Creation, covenant, and exodus; incarnation, resurrection, and the Pentecostal outpouring of the Spirit; the saving reign of God as present fact and eschatological hope—everything we believe and everything we preach involves the "mighty acts" of God.

The most commonly recognizable manifestations of these acts take place in what the church calls "sacraments," where God's action *intersects* human actions without either *interrupting* or *interfering* with them. In baptism, eucharist, confirmation, ordination, marriage, reconciliation, and anointing, grace translates human word and gesture into something more than mere social ritual. Sacraments, we believe, are ways by which God convenes and nurtures the Christian community and brings in the reign of peace and justice that no human agency alone can effect.

These "official acts," however, do not exhaust the range of God's *modus operandi*. Sacraments provide a context within which we can recognize and respond to God's other actions, which are often subtle and sometimes highly personal occasions of grace. Each of us is "marked as Christ's own forever" in baptism. The distinctive meaning and shape of that mark, however, only becomes clear to us over time as we reflect on influential factors and turning points in the course of our lives. The discovery of how God loves me distinctively is an awesome experience.

One of the primary tasks of preaching is to help individuals and communities discover the countless ways in which through grace they are constantly being

- marked as Christ's own (which we celebrate most explicitly in baptism);
- nourished by Christ's life (which we experience tangibly at each eucharist);
- incorporated into Christ's Body by its other members (upon which the rite of confirmation dwells most particularly);
- called into special service (of which ordination is a dramatic symbol);

∽ brought into significant human relationships (which marriage is one way of honoring);

∽ forgiven and healed in the midst of all our relationships (which we vividly celebrate in the rites of reconciliation and unction).

Each of the sacraments expresses, in a liturgical context, one of these particular dimensions of God's grace that is working among us all the time. Good preaching draws attention to the sacramental dimension of our lives.

But preaching does much more than just talk about sacraments. When Archbishop of Canterbury Donald Coggin described preaching as "the sacrament of the word," he meant that the sermon word, which focuses our attention on God's distinctive actions of grace in our lives, is itself a graceful act of God. The utterance of God's word always gives light. Naming a truth can make it true.

All preaching calls attention to the extraordinary in the presence of the everyday. It seeks to show us where and how, as Gerard Manley Hopkins says, "the world is charged with the grandeur of God." Preaching upon special occasions (however we define them) can never aim at *less* than this. A sermon always holds the potential for discerning God's action and formulating our response. This basic task is our responsibility *anytime* we are in the pulpit, "in season and out of season," as Paul says to Timothy.

Not all the days of our lives (from our own perspectives, at least) are equally "high times," nor can we make them such. In the normal course of the meals we take, there is necessary daily nourishment—sometimes a hurried nibble or a light snack, sometimes a modest lunch, sometimes a sit-down dinner with nothing fancy. But there are also times for banquets: a wild party, a fancy celebration, or a solemn formal occasion. Each of these different meals has its place; each entails a different way of preparing the table and participating in table fellowship. It is awkward if someone tries to fix us a fancy breakfast when we are already late for an appointment, or about to go out for a morning run: "Just a piece of toast, a glass of juice, and a cup of coffee, please! Don't go to any trouble!" There is not much glory in preparing a simple meal. But there is great need for the preparation of such fare—much more need, in fact, than there is for a banquet.

It is, however, every bit as awkward to arrive for a meal at an occasion (say, a graduation, a silver wedding anniversary, Thanksgiving, Christmas, or Easter) when a festive preparation is clearly called for, only to find that little care has been taken to honor the occasion. "Care" is the operative word here. It does not take extravagance or culinary virtuosity to honor a special occasion, only competence joined with intentionality. I shall never forget such a meal in the mountains of Guatemala. My fellow visitors and I were each served a fried egg—a rare delicacy our Mayan Indian hosts could ill afford. They were offering us their hospitality, and we were indeed honored by the care they took in preparing for and celebrating our visit in this way.

Sermons on special occasions should not be ostentatious, for then they will subvert their own purposes—much like the elaborate meals that are not so much fancy as fussy. Just as faithful "everyday" preaching will exercise care to see that the nourishment appropriate for those occasions is fittingly presented, faithful special occasion preaching will be marked by an unmistakable quality of care that can meet the expectations of those who gather to hear us preach: "This day is different! Is there a word from the Lord for us on a day like this?"

As preachers, we are charged with helping people experience the continuity of God's creativity in their lives. We focus on distinctive expressions of God's grace and give particular focus to those expressions—on a special occasion and on any occasion—so that listeners can continue to seek their place in the unfolding of God's grace in their lives. Faithful preaching will preach *through* any situation, using the gospel as a lens and a lantern: a lens through which to see the occasion in fresh perspective, and a lantern to provide a sense of direction. In this way listeners will be able to sense for themselves that, in the words of a prayer used on Good Friday and at ordinations: "things which were cast down are being raised up, and things which had grown old are being made new, and that all things are being brought to their perfection by him through whom all things were made."